Rail Freight
– today

No. 47319 Norsk Hydro in Speedlink Distribution sub sector livery, heads a train of empty Norsk Cargowaggons through Brocklesby on 7th July 1988.

Rail Freight
– today

by

C.R. Anthony & B. Rogers

Oxford Publishing Co.

A FOULIS-OPC Railway Book

British Library Cataloguing in Publication Data
Rogers, B.
  Railfreight today.
  I. Great Britain. Railway freight transport
  services. British Rail. Freight
  I. Title   II. Anthony, C.R.
  385'.24'0941
  ISBN 0-86093-439-X

Library of Congress catalog card number
  88-82694

Published by:
Haynes Publishing Group
Sparkford, near Yeovil, Somerset BA22 7JJ.

Haynes Publications Inc.
861 Lawrence Drive, Newbury Park, California 91320, USA.

Printed by J.H. Haynes & Co. Ltd.

Frontispiece:
Class 45 No. 45108 passes Kilnhurst with the empty Dewsbury to Hope Cemflo wagons, on 22nd June 1987.

On 19th February 1987 Nos 20174 and 20173 arrive at Wilton with a trip working from Tees Yard. It is made up of three VDA wagons used for adepic acid traffic to Bridgwater, and a butadiene tank wagon. The latter traffic, from King's Lynn, now moves by road.

Contents

Acknowledgements

A.V. Dawson Ltd
Appleton Associates
B.P. Chemicals Ltd
British Alcan Aluminium Ltd
British Coal
British Oxygen Company Ltd
British Steel
British Sugar PLC
Blue Circle Industries PLC
CAIB UK Ltd
C.E.G.B.
Ciba-Geigy Chemicals Ltd
Cleveland Bridge and Engineering Ltd
Cleveland Potash Ltd
Cobra Railfreight Ltd
Colas Roads Ltd
Courtaulds Ltd
Croda Hydrocarbons Ltd
D & F Steels Ltd
Dunlop Ranken
Egger UK Ltd
Freightliners Ltd
Hargreaves Scotland
ICI Chemicals & Polymers Ltd
Isis Link Ltd
Immingham Port Authority
Immingham Railfreight Terminals
John G. Russell (Transport) Ltd
Leeds Oil Rail Terminal
Mineralhaul Ltd
Norsk Hydro Fertilizers
Peakstone Ltd

Peter D. Stirling Ltd
Plasmor
Port of Tyne Authority
Procor Engineering Ltd
RFS Engineering
Redland Roof Tiles Ltd
Revell Fuels
Ridsdale & Walker
Rockware Glass Ltd
Scunthorpe Rod Mill
Selby Storage & Freight Co. Ltd
Shell Oil Terminal (Jarrow)
Simon Storage Group
Standard Railfreight
Steetley Quarry Products Ltd
Stockton Haulage Ltd
Tees & Hartlepool Port Authority
Thompsons of Prudhoe Ltd
Tilcon
Tioxide UK Ltd
UKF Fertilizers
United Engineering Steels
VTG (UK) Ltd
Viking Shipping
Western Softwoods Ltd
Wimpey Waste Management Ltd

British Rail Management.
British Rail staff at Tyne, Tees, Belmont, Tinsley & Healey Mills.
British Rail TOPS Office Middlesbrough.
British Rail Speedlink Office, York.

A special thank you to all members of British Rail staff and private company employees who have contributed to this book. All photographs were taken by the authors.

Introduction

One has only to look at the railway section in libraries and bookshops to realise that the humble freight train takes second place to the speedier and more glamorous passenger train.

The general public, and indeed those interested in railways, have always been inevitably drawn to the thoroughbreds—the A1s, A4s, Kings, Duchesses, Westerns and Deltics—rather than to the workhorses of the system. And yet, just as the former have disappeared from the railway scene, so the loco-hauled passenger train is quickly becoming a thing of the past in many parts of the country. As the new-generation electric and diesel multiple units gradually take over, locomotive-hauled trains on cross-country and Provincial services are fading into history.

There will still be electric locomotives on the East Coast and West Coast Main Lines, but diesels on passenger workings will be few and far between. It is not surprising, therefore, that in the last couple of years there has been an upsurge of interest in freight. It is the purpose of this book to foster this interest by describing what can be seen today, taking the North East area as an example. As well as outlining freight movements, we have also tried to put the British Rail operations in context by linking them with the industries they serve. Wagons are an important part of any freight handling and we have, where possible, attempted to show these clearly in the photographs. The range of goods carried by Railfreight is still considerable, the scene today being made even more interesting by the variety of locomotive liveries and symbols, and the colours, shapes and types of wagons on the network.

A word about two items dealt with in this book. First, Section 8 grants. These became available under Section 8 of the 1974 Railways Act and were intended to cover part of the capital cost of rail freight facilities where the transfer of freight from road to rail would improve the community environment. A grant could also be secured if a rail-served company continued to use rail and if the same environmental criteria were met. The grants, which may be up to 50% of the capital cost, can be used for sidings, equipment and wagons.

Second, locomotive dedication. The initial intention was to transfer a given number of Class 20, 37 and 47 locomotives to Thornaby in November 1986. Allocated to the Metals sub-sector of Railfreight, they were to be used almost exclusively on Metals trains. The dedication to a particular traffic flow would reduce re-allocations between depots and virtually eliminate re-allocations between sub-sectors, for example, Metals to Oil. Dedication has now spread to the other sub-sectors, but the 'ring fence' policy has been modified and is no longer adhered to as rigidly as was first conceived. The original Metals experiment appears to have been successful, especially the pairing of locomotives on a long-term basis. (See Metals chapter.)

Although dealing primarily with the North East, the area has not been looked at in isolation, and where appropriate, other regions have been brought in. In the main, the book covers the years 1987/88 and although not an exhaustive enquiry, it is hoped that it is an accurate picture of those years.

Finally, we should like to thank the staff of the companies we have visited. Their cheerful assistance has been much appreciated. But without the help, guidance, tolerance, knowledge and good humour of British Rail personnel, this book could not have been written.

50-60 trains a day discharge coal at Drax in a 24 hour operation. As many as 10 trains can be accommodated at any one time on the power station layout.

Chapter 1

Trainload Coal

"Even the stationmaster used to sell coal"

The importance of coal to Britain's economy can hardly be overstressed. Although the days when every halt and siding held at least one coal wagon are long gone, coal is still an important element of Britain's industrial strategy. We talk about coal in terms of millions of tonnes and indeed it is the fuel which generates three-quarters of all our electricity.

The growth of new industries after 1945 meant that the local urban power stations were pressed to supply the amount of electricity required and the then Central Electricity Authority decided to build large coal-burning stations close to rivers and major coalfields. The giant stations of Eggborough, Ferrybridge and Drax were built in the Aire Valley and although some coal comes in from the North East, they are mainly served by Yorkshire pits. Drax, midway between Goole and Selby, is the largest coal-fired power station in Western Europe. Its weekly winter burn is approximately 250,000 tonnes and can be more over the Christmas period. It is not surprising, therefore, that with these vast tonnages rail was the obvious choice for moving the coal from pit to power station. Drax, for example, is served from a number of Yorkshire and North East pits, the largest of which is Selby.

If we take a typical mgr trip from Kellingley we see that the full train comprises 36 HAA wagons and is hauled by a Class 56 locomotive. On arrival at the colliery the slow-running gear is engaged whilst the train passes beneath the twelve outlets of the 3,000 tonne bunker at 1mph. These outlets are worked by two cabin operators. The total loading time is fifteen to twenty minutes and the train is automatically weighed both tare and gross. The locomotive then has to uncouple and run round its loaded wagons. The trip to Drax is short and on arrival the train may have to wait whilst others are being unloaded. Drax has the facilities for discharging three trains simultaneously and because British Rail makes full use of permissive signalling, it is possible to have as many as ten trains on the vast layout there.

The lines into the power station and the loop belong to the CEGB but are maintained by British Rail. Again, the slow-running gear is engaged, the levers on the wagons are tripped by 'daleks' and the coal floods onto underground conveyors which take it either for immediate burn or for stockpiling. The range of time to discharge is a variable depending upon weather conditions and quality of coal, although the objective is to achieve approximately 40 minutes. Sometimes, however, the coal is not right. It may have too much shale content, it may be too wet. In the latter case there is a tendency to get a build-up of coal on the rail which can cause problems. The Class 56 locomotives do slip in extreme conditions and the use of sand is essential. British Rail carried out tests with an air blaster in front of the locomotive wheels to break off the shale and give it a better grip. However it was felt that by using air pressure from the locomotive for the blaster there was a possibility that the efficiency of the braking system might be affected. Experiments are now to be carried out with a static air blaster.

After the doors have been closed, each wagon is inspected as it leaves and any cripples removed. Every train passing through unloads on average 1,100 tonnes and there are 50 to 60 trains a day. It is a 24 hour operation and trains arrive from 22.00 on a Sunday until midday on Saturday. Should problems arise, it is often cheaper and more convenient to send the coal on to another power station rather than have a protracted hold-up. From the CEGB's point of view, the shorter the haul the cheaper the cost. Coal brought in from Durham, for example, proves very expensive and as far as Drax is concerned the Selby Coalfield cannot come on full stream too soon. When this happens, it will supply Drax with up to 180,000 tonnes a week, all of which will be transported by British Rail.

The mgr principle, simple enough in theory, needs detailed organisation and close cooperation for it to function efficiently. British Rail liaises closely with the CEGB and British Coal at national, regional and local level. British Coal decides how much coal is available for the following week and at which pits. The CEGB specifies the tonnage required and the power stations to be served and British Rail indicates its ability to move the coal and decides how many locomotives and wagons are needed. A plan is then produced on computer. Dialogue also takes place at local level on a day to day basis, for it would be unreasonable to assume that when one million tonnes a week are being shifted on Eastern Region that no problems arise. Locomotives can fail, crews can go sick, a train may arrive at a pit and find that unavoidably, no coal is available. The power station might not be able to discharge quickly enough or the 'daleks' may not be working properly. The advantage of having a large bunker at the pit is that the capacity is there to put things right. Similarly the power station has large stockpiles of coal.

The bulk of mgr coal moves through the power stations at $1/2$mph, but there are now agreements with British Coal to load the coal at 1mph at certain pits, of which Kellingley is one. There is also the technology for trains to be loaded and unloaded unmanned. For instance, Eggborough was the test-bed for the 'wiggly-wire' system. This is a wire placed between the rails. As the locomotive passes over, it is controlled by messages transmitted through the wire. The object is to allow the driver to take his personal needs break without having to have an additional driver as a stand-in. Two locomotives, Nos 56073 and 56074 are the only ones fitted with the equipment to work Eggborough and can be recognised by the light on the cab roof. British Rail now regards this sytem as obsolete and tests are at present being carried out with the radio control of locomotives through the power stations. The safety aspect is at the forefront of all railway thinking and before introducing new technology, BR must be convinced of its safety. In addition, close cooperation with the rail unions is necessary to get agreement and acceptance.

In principle, all northern pits have mgr facilities. But not all pits use the overhead bunker method for loading the wagons; Kiverton Park and Seaham use the pad method. At Seaham the loading takes place by means of two front-loading Michigan 275B shovels. Each shovel takes six wagons and moves along the 360-400 yard concrete pad until the 36-wagon train is fully loaded. This can, in fact, be almost as quick as the overhead method. Seaham Colliery is an interesting example. Up to Christmas 1986 the bulk of the coal was loaded into the old 21 tonne HTV hopper wagons by traditional methods under the screens and was then sent to South Dock, Sunderland, for shipment. The layout has been changed and the pit has been converted to rapid loading facilities by pad. The coal is now put into HAA

Class 56 No. 56094 stops at the loading bunker to engage the slow speed control at Kellingley Colliery on 26th November 1986.

wagons and can go either to Tyne Coal Terminal or any of the CEGB power stations.

At some Yorkshire pits a 'mule' is used instead of the locomotive to take the wagons through the loading area. At the time of writing discussions are going on with British Coal with a view to having the 'mules' taken out and allowing the locomotive to haul the wagons through the bunkers.

Generally speaking, BR faces little competition when moving coal to power stations. What competition there is usually comes from the barge and coastal shipping, rather than the old enemy, the heavy lorry. At Kellingley Colliery coal is delivered along the River Aire to Ferrybridge C in three pansets, 500 tonnes at a time. On arrival these are hoisted out of the water and tipped. Barges, the old 'Tom Puddings', take coal to Ferrybridge B, though a typical load is only about 170 tonnes. In total about 1,200 tonnes are sent each week by river, which is not much more than one BR merry-go-round train, and if the river rises because of rain, the pansets cannot get under the Aire Bridge which carries the A1!

The new Tyne Coal Terminal (TCT), owned and operated by the Port of Tyne Authority, has replaced all but one of the British Rail staithes in the North East. With their closure have gone the smaller wagons, the HTVs and HUOs. Constructed at a cost of £12 million and opened in 1985, the terminal is able to handle up to 14 trains a day over two shifts through a rapid discharge system. Now taking the lion's share of coal shipments from Durham, a high proportion is sent to the Thames Valley power stations at West Thurrock, Tilbury and Kingsnorth. In addition, a significant volume is exported to EEC and Scandanavian destinations. Discussions are now being held at the Port of Tyne to open the terminal over three shifts. In August 1988 the Westoe pit is to be rail-connected and the coal will be sent to TCT. There will then be in the order of 21 trains going to TCT over three shifts.

The only remaining British Rail staithe is to be found at Blyth, and this, too, is coming to the end of its working life. Completed in 1928 and with a length of 1,600ft, the West Staithe can berth two ships, or one larger vessel, and has 30ft of water at low tide. The timber below the water mark is American greenheart which is virtually impervious to water.

The working here is fascinating. Coal trains come into the West Yard at Cambois where the locomotive uncouples. The wagons are then pushed by shunting pilot in groups of ten to the end of the staithes. They are then allowed to gravitate slowly down over the discharge point where they are stopped and the bottom doors manually opened. The coal teems out into a hopper and passes by means of a chute onto the conveyor belt and into the ship itself. The men on the stage are called 'teemers' and are employed by British Rail. Much of the coal is sent to Northern Ireland but there are shipments to France, West Germany, Denmark and Portugal. The amount of traffic brought by BR to the staithes depends to a large extent on the price of oil. If the latter is high, the demand for coal goes up. The second variable for BR is the amount of coal British Coal has to allocate. When the oil price is low and there is a loss of market for mined coal, BR is vulnerable. Potentially $1\frac{1}{2}$ to 2 million tonnes could be shipped each year from the West Staithes, but the actual figure is nearer 1 million tonnes.

The other shipment point is Blyth Bates. Owned by British Coal, the rail link was severed as the local colliery was running down towards closure. Although the Bates terminal is road-fed at the moment, there is an application in for a Section 8 grant. The old line will not take the newer HAA wagons so the curvature between Newsham and Bates will have to be realigned to allow access to locomotives and wagons. A rapid discharge facility must also be put in before it can be rail-connected. The earliest possible opening date is October 1989.

An interesting movement, and one for which British Rail has signed a 10 year contract is from Blyth to Ellesmere Port on Merseyside. Despatched in distinctive yellow purpose-built wagons and containers, the high quality fuel is shipped from the container terminal in Ellesmere Port for distribution in Northern Ireland. The agreement is for 2 million tonnes a year and the 6M21 leaves Blyth at 09.55 (MSX). The Saturday train departs at 02.34.

Not strictly a Railfreight movement, but well worthy of mention, is the procedure at Harton near Jarrow. The British Coal staithes here are fed from Westoe Colliery by a private electric railway in wagons known as 'reds'. These are the conventional type of loose-coupled hopper wagons. Although Westoe is a large pit, the staithes limit the size of

The 36 HAA wagons are loaded at Kellingley in about 15 minutes whilst the train is travelling at 1 mph. Most systems operate with the train travelling at $^1/_2$ mph.

Having run round its train, No. 56094 heads out of the colliery bound for Drax Power Station.

On the 17th November 1986, No. 56103 waits on the loop line at Drax to enter the discharge area.

No. 56094 enters the unloading area. The slow speed control is selected and the 'daleks' (the boxes on the left of the locomotive) trip the wagon doors to discharge the coal down the grates.

vessel which can berth there. Since ships' demurrage is very expensive, British Coal have to have a lot of their own wagons already filled and waiting so that on arrival the ships can be loaded quickly. The coal is high quality and tends to be for CEGB power stations. One and a half to two million tonnes per annum is shipped. As previously mentioned British Coal are intending modernising the terminal facilities at Westoe and providing for the movement of the coal in HAA wagons hauled by British Rail to Tyne Coal Terminal. (The coal staithes at Harton have now closed.)

A recent gain for BR is ICI Wilton's conversion of two of its oil-burning boilers to coal. The first coal train arrived at the newly-installed mgr facility in September 1986. Beginning with one train a day, this is now two, the deliveries being at approximately 06.30 and 18.30. Eleven hundred tonne trains deliver the coal in exactly the same way as at a CEGB power station. Most of the coal comes from Butterwell in Northumberland. If the coal is to go to the bunkers, it goes straight up the conveyor belt. Should the

From the sunken hut between the tracks, the wagons are examined to check that the discharge doors are all closed and that there are no defective wagons.

The 'wiggly wire' (between the tracks) at Eggborough was the system tried by British Rail to run locomotives through the discharge point unmanned, thus enabling the crew to take their meal break away from the locomotive.

bunkers be full, the first arm of the giant reclaimer spreads it around the stockpile. If there is no coal in the bunkers, the second arm takes it from the pile and it is conveyed straight to the boilers.

Another interesting coal movement is to the Hope Valley. Blue Circle Cement there take about three trains a week for firing the cement kilns. British Rail are also optimistic in securing a similar tonnage in HAAs to the same company in Dunbar.

The transportation of coke and coking coal, which in former years provided BR with a substantial revenue, has decreased considerably. The British Steel Corporation was in recent times one of the prime users of coke, but with the decline in steel making capacity, the market has declined. The loss of foundry capacity has again had a negative effect and, of course, the domestic market is subject to competition from alternative fuels such as oil and natural gas. This marked reduction in coal and coke requirements was accelerated by the NUM strike. Of the coking plants in the North East, only Monkton near Jarrow now remains.

On 7th July 1987, No. 56127 waits with its train at Seaham Colliery whilst the HAA wagons are loaded by mechanical shovel.

The Michigan mechanical shovels can load a train almost as quickly as the overhead bunker method. This type of loading is known as pad loading.

One of Railfreight's competitors in the movement of power station coal from Kellingley is barge traffic on the River Aire. Here a 'Tom Pudding' is loaded at Kellingley's wharf – movement is to the nearby Ferrybridge Power Station.

Tyne Coal Terminal, operated by the Port of Tyne Authority, exports coal to EEC countries and Scandinavia, as well as supplying CEGB power stations in the Thames Valley. Having run from Widdrington, No. 56114 hauls its 36 HAAs through the discharge point on the 9th October 1987.

The coal staithe at Blyth, built in 1928, is of timber construction. Wagons are shunted to the end of the staithe and descend by gravity to the discharge point near the ship. The bottom doors are operated manually by the 'teemers'.

Domestic coal moves in Cawood's containers from Ellington Colliery to Ellesmere Port for shipment to Ireland. No. 56118 passes Bolton Percy with the distinctive yellow container train.

A second coal staithe on the Tyne, but owned by British Coal, is at Harton. The wagons are moved from Westoe Colliery to the staithe along the British Coal owned electric railway.

No. 56125 enters Tyne Yard on 18th June 1987 with a loaded coal train from the Swalwell open cast site. The locomotive runs round the train to gain the line to Blyth Power Station.

Coking coal from Orgreave, Sheffield, was until recently moved in HTV wagons to Scunthorpe. The coke is loaded hot and allowed to cool whilst the wagons stand in the exchange sidings.

Coke in HEA wagons moves from Orgreave to Scunthorpe. Class 56 No. 56101 approaches Thorne Junction bound for Scunthorpe on 14th July 1988.

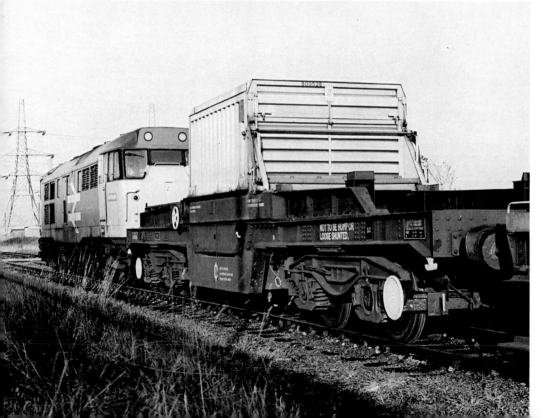

On the 14th October 1987, Class 31 No. 31163 hauls what was only the second train of spent nuclear fuel to leave Hartlepool Power Station. The flasks travel to Sellafield where the fuel is re-processed.

A Class 56 locomotive, the work horse of the pit to power station coal trains, passes Ferrybridge, one of the Aire Valley power stations.

Unfortunately the coal delivered from the nearby Wearmouth pit comes in by road since the rail facility is not suitable for HAAs.

In the south of the area, coke produced at Orgreave is taken to British Steel Scunthorpe daily by rail. Originally hauled by two Class 20s in HTVs, the coke is now delivered in HEAs by a Class 56. HAA wagons were tried but BR found that the larger lumps of coke got under the horns on the doors, preventing them from opening. The problem was solved by using the HEAs which are manually operated. After the miners' dispute a low-volatile coal from Betteshanger in Kent, which was used to get the blend correct, went over to road but British Rail has now won this back. About 20,000 tonnes a week are moved from Yorkshire collieries plus a further 10,000 tonnes of the special coal from Betteshanger and Oakdale in South Wales.

Colliery waste such as shale is occasionally moved by BR but because of the high cost of moving a product which is virtually valueless, except for landfill, British Coal is naturally reluctant to involve BR. However, BR has won a contract to convey 10,000 tonnes of shale a week from local collieries to Seaham Harbour in HAAs.

A sensitive issue with political and ecological overtones is that of acid rain, yet it is one which is likely to benefit British Rail considerably. Emissions from coal-fired power stations are thought to be a major cause of acid rain. The sulphur dioxide and nitrogen dioxide in the emissions mix with the moisture in the atmosphere to produce dilute sulphuric and nitric acids. When it rains, the rain can be acidic, polluting rivers and lakes, and damaging vegetation. In an attempt to solve this problem Drax Power Station is to have a desulphurisation plant installed and this will mean the delivery of vast tonnages of limestone. A conservative estimate is 600/700,000 tonnes per annum. The limestone will be crushed, treated and the chimney fumes sprayed with limewater to neutralize the acidity. This gas scrubbing plant, or scrubber, will produce a residue. Depending upon the type of scrubber installed, sulphurs and sulphuric acid or gypsum will be produced. It is understood that the Drax plant will produce gypsum. This in turn will present BR with a commercial opportunity as large amounts will have to be removed. The only problem for BR, though one eminently soluble, is the dovetailing of the coal and limestone movements. Remember that Drax has 50 plus mgrs a day! Should future legislation require that all coal-fired power stations install scrubbers, then BR could be onto a real winner.

It may seem unusual at this point to mention nuclear fuels, but their marketing and transport comes under coal business as far as British Rail is concerned. There is a contract with the CEGB, and BR simply act as transporter. They are informed where and when the flasks are to be moved and act accordingly. In late 1987 Hartlepool Power Station at Seaton began sending nuclear fuel to Sellafield for reprocessing. Nationally there are about 50 flask movements a year and there is no doubt that the railways are the safest transporter of these fuels. The high profile destruction of Class 46 No. 46009 in 1984 was certainly spectacular and achieved the desired effect of showing that the 48 tonne flasks could withstand a high-speed crash and remain intact.

Certainly the transportation of coal in percentage terms is by far the biggest sub-sector in the freight business. There are, however, some incipient problems. It is not too simplistic to say that the size of the coal industry is determined by the CEGB. As transporter of the coal, British Rail could be vulnerable. One has only to think back to the NUM strike where the railways are said to have lost £400 million in revenues. Coking plants have closed. British Steel now imports a substantial tonnage which is a loss to British Coal. In many instances, however, BR has managed to secure the movement but it is true to say that some traffic is still moved by road. The rebuilt coal terminal at Immingham is again operational and is fortunately rail-connected. This facility is used exclusively for export, imports being brought in at Immingham Bulk Terminal where the iron ore is also imported. Should a privatised CEGB decide, however, to fire its power stations with cheaper foreign coal imports, British Rail could lose revenue from British pits. Fortunately this should not prove too detrimental since environmental issues would almost certainly preclude the use of road transport to deliver the coal from port to power station. British Rail is the only alternative.

Chapter 2

Speedlink Coal

Traditionally coal merchants used to receive traffic in conventional flat-bottom 16 ton mineral or 21 ton hopper wagons. In past decades thousands of such wagons trundled around the network, frequently being used as storage by dealers in their yards. Several factors came together to focus the need for a reappraisal of the transport of domestic coal. First was the implementation of Beeching's policy to get rid of inefficient and unprofitable wagonload traffic. Then came the natural decline of coal and coke in the 1960s and 70s due to the discovery of natural gas and the availability of cheap oil. The final factor was that the 16 and 21 ton wagons were by the end of the 1970s over 25 years old and needed replacing.

A choice had to be made as to whether British Rail should withdraw completely from wagonload coal traffic or whether money should be invested in a new wagon for the future. Fortunately, in the early 1980s, the decision was taken to replace the conventional wagon with a high-capacity wagon capable of travelling at speeds similar to passenger trains. This would mean only a minimum of inconvenience to the passenger network. Thus the older, obsolete wagons were phased out over a period of time and the HEA wagon introduced. The latter is capable of travelling at 60 mph.

The post-Beeching era had seen the introduction of the coal concentration depot. The closure of station yards led to traffic being concentrated at a certain point, this point becoming known as the coal concentration depot (CCD). An initial difficulty arose in persuading the coal merchants to use the CCDs. Naturally enough, the latter saw themselves as independent, for when they received coal in the 16 ton mineral wagons, they received it in their own name, and they would discharge it themselves. British Rail had therefore to get the individual dealers to see the benefits of the CCD by showing them it was cost effective. They would no longer have to employ staff to bag the coal. In the CCD they would either receive it bagged, or if they so chose, in bulk.

The majority of the CCDs became operational between 1965 and 1970. They were built typically with a throughput capacity of between 75,000 and 150,000 tons, but because of the previously mentioned conversions to gas and oil, plus the introduction of smokeless zones, the amount of fuel dealt with is now considerably less.

The streamlining of domestic coal deliveries was not achieved without blood-letting. The year 1982 saw the withdrawal of rail connections to most of the 292 coal depots throughout mainland Britain, and by 1986 the total number of rail-connected depots had shrunk to about 70.

It was originally intended to convert fully to Speedlink by 1986 but the cut over date was brought forward by two years, theoretically to 1st May 1984. These good intentions did not, however, foresee the miners' strike and in reality March 1985 would be a more accurate date. Again, the strike meant not only a loss of traffic but also a loss of confidence in that BR crews refused to handle the traffic that was available. There is no doubt that some of the traffic lost to road haulage has never been recovered. On the brighter side, however, Speedlink coal was to be moved long distances using the normal Speedlink services. Feeder services were to operate from the colliery to the marshalling yard. Trunk haulage would deliver the coal to another, perhaps distant, marshalling yard, from where trip services would take it to its destination. The trunk haul was usually overnight and it was expected that traffic released from a colliery one day would be at its destination the next, certainly after two at the very latest.

It was not long, however, before the new Speedlink Coal service came once again under scrutiny, the problem being the profitability of running coal on general Speedlink services geared to pre-NUM strike tonnage of domestic fuel. Before the dispute, 2¹/₂ million tonnes were moved, the figure now being 1¹/₄ million. The costs of running the services are allocated to all the commodity sectors that put traffic on those services. An exercise was carried out to ascertain whether costs could best be contained by

The backbone of Speedlink coal movements is the 45 tonne HEA hopper wagon. No. 361338 is depicted.

On 1st June 1987, No. 47238 leaves the Speedlink coal trunk yard at Healey Mills with a train of HEA hopper wagons.

Class 45 No. 45041 leaves Kellingley on the 17th November 1986 with a train of FPA coal container wagons.

Household coal for John G. Russell's west of Scotland customers moves to Gartcosh in FPA container wagons.

The containers are lifted from the FPA wagons by large container handling vehicles.

Fleets of lorries wait for the arrival of the trains. The containers are then transferred to the road vehicles for delivery to customers in the west of Scotland.

Class 37 No. 37176 collects an empty HEA wagon from the Sculcoates coal concentration depot (CCD) at Hull on the 6th April 1987.

Staff at Sculcoates use a donkey engine and wire rope to haul the wagons over the discharge pit.

Anthracite from South Wales is discharged at the Hull Calvert Lane coal concentration depot. The anthracite moves on conveyor from the discharge pit to the waiting road vehicle.

providing a separate service for coal. They already had the wagons. If both locomotives and human resources were put at their disposal, there would be scope to provide specific accountability for the coal activity. A further argument was that the Speedlink services often did not fit in well with where the coal was wanting to go. The outcome was the setting up of the Speedlink Coal Network which became fully operational in July 1987. Many of the smaller unremunerative trip services were dispensed with and the trains shared facilities with trainload coal. In the North, Healey Mills became a trunk yard specialising in both trainload and wagonload coal. Feeder services arrive from Brodsworth, Grimethorpe Coalite, Kellingley, Markham Main and Monckton, and trunk haulage is to Gartcosh, Hull and Preston via Blackburn.

Because Yorkshire is especially rich in high-quality bituminous housecoal, there is a heavy flow to Preston in the North West and especially to Scotland. We have already noted that rural Scotland does not have the supplies of natural gas that England enjoys. Add to this the independence of the Scottish coal merchants and we have the ingredients for the second method of delivering Speedlink coal, namely the container. Most of the containerised coal goes to a road haulier, John G. Russell of Gartcosh near Glasgow. The company is part of the Scottish domestic coal distribution system whereby British Coal is able to supplement the output of Scottish pits to meet the local demand. Quick to see the advantages of containerised coal by rail, Russell's applied for and won a Section 8 grant in 1982. The fuel is loaded at the colliery into 30ft long by 6ft 6in high steel or aluminium containers and travels overnight to Scotland on FPA wagons. Since it is known in advance how many containers are to arrive, the company is able to have the requisite number of lorries waiting for immediate

despatch to the coal merchants. The containers have rear doors, therefore once transferred by heavy lifting trucks from train to lorry, they can easily be tipped where and when required. The Scottish merchants seem to prefer this one load/one tip arrangement as the coal arrives quickly in prime condition.

Russell's are also able to store the coal in two ways. The containers can be stacked four high in the considerable space available, or they can be tipped out onto an existing stockpile for later reclamation. Normally about 5,000 tonnes of coal are held at the end of the summer months. From Gartcosh the coal is mainly delivered to the west of Scotland, their depots at Inverness and Aberdeen giving coverage to the rest of Scotland. Depending on the type of product, a container holds up to 26 tonnes of housecoal, but it is restricted to 24 tonnes to meet the permissible gross weight for road deliveries. This compares favourably with the HEA which carries about 23 tonnes of coal or anthracite, 16 tonnes of Rexco, 17 tonnes of Sunbrite but only 14 tonnes of coke.

British Rail has the capability of running two trains a day to Scotland. The customer can order coal weekly and expect British Coal to make the fuel available on a regular basis. Problems at Yorkshire pits in the post-strike months, however, meant that British Coal could not meet the demand and Russell's in fact never received the full requirement. In general, only one train ran instead of two.

A further link in the Scottish connection is Peter D. Sirling Ltd of Mossend. Again a road haulier has seen the advantage of links with Railfreight and their site, ideally situated next to Mossend Yard, accepts all kinds of railborne products. Domestic coal is received from Yorkshire and South Wales in HEA wagons and is transferred to road vehicle via a highly efficient purpose-built conveyor system and a large capacity cell. A wagon can be unloaded in three minutes and there is also a facility to stockpile. The Speedlink Coal service is geared to move up to 400,000 tonnes of fuel a year from English and Welsh pits to Scotland, a considerable percentage of this coming from North East England. It is reckoned that about 10,000 heavy lorry loads are kept off British roads each year in this way.

A further gain from road is the trial Speedlink Coal operation which transports coalite from Grimethorpe in Yorkshire direct to Mossend, Glasgow. Hargreaves, the Scottish Coalite subsidiary, have a rail-connected depot next to the Speedlink yard. From there the coalite is distributed throughout Scotland by road. What makes this rail movement particularly interesting is that it takes place on a Sunday. The trains are scheduled to leave Grimethorpe at 09.56 (6S42) and 12.30 (6S43) and arrive at Mossend at 20.13 and 00.43 respectively. The HEAs are discharged by a Freeland Mobile FC280 unloader conveyor on the 'under wagon, over rail' principle. The trial began in February 1987 and continued until April 1988. Hargreaves were happy with the arrangement and the scheme continues to operate. Hargreaves also handle bituminous fuels which arrive for the most part from Manton, Rufford, Kellingley and Markham collieries. It is hoped that these coal and coalite movements, plus the company's central situation and convenient type of operation, will help reverse the decline in the demand for domestic solid fuel.

When Freightliners closed their Aberdeen container terminal in May 1987, few people would have expected it to become the focal point of an exciting new Speedlink Coal initiative. Yet this is exactly what occurred. With Russell's and Aberdeen Coal, Railfreight has adapted the site to handle containerised loads. The coal, which comes predo-

minantly from the Yorkshire coalfields, is sent up the East Coast Main Line, thus generating some new traffic for British Rail which was formerly in the hands of road hauliers.

In the North there are coal concentration depots at Lincoln, Grimsby and Hull, where there are two. The needs of Lincoln and Grimsby do not justify a full Speedlink Coal delivery and are therefore served by a service shared with other Speedlink traffics. The two Hull depots are larger, however, and from Monday to Thursday 6L59 leaves Healey Mills at 19.20 arriving in Hull Dairycoates at 20.55. The following morning the wagons are tripped to Hull Sculcoates and Hull Calvert Lane. The former is run by Revell Fuels, the latter by Ridsdale and Walker. The total stocking capacity of both companies is considerable, each being in the region of 10,000 tonnes.

Not all fuels are railborne, however, since some originating points do not have a railhead. Also, where British pits cannot meet local needs, for example, anthracite, some product is imported. The sites are rented from BR on the basis that the companies take most of their requirement by rail. This they are happy to do since rail is competitive to the depots. Most of the household coal comes from Yorkshire pits and is discharged into a below-rail hopper system. From there it is taken to bagging hoppers or loaded directly into road vehicles. The two Hull depots' annual railborne traffic is about 20,000 tonnes and has a weekly variation of between 200 and 800 tonnes.

The change-over to the Speedlink Coal Network has proved very successful and has been well received by the trade. The latter now sees a situation where Speedlink Coal is offering a better and more flexible service than previously.

Healey Mills Yard near Dewsbury has become a trunk yard for both trainload and Speedlink coal.

Chapter 3

Oil

Although the railways have carried oil since the last century, it was not until after the Second World War that it became a large scale commodity for transport. The market really took off in the late 1950s and early 1960s with the introduction of the supertankers bringing in Middle Eastern oil at low cost. The growth in the number of motorcars increased the demand and in the early 1960s the concept of the modern diesel-hauled high capacity oil train was born. Industry invested heavily in reception and unloading terminals and the railway took a significant share of the transportation market. Such was the confidence in those years that rail contracts with the oil companies could be for as long as 20 years, but most were for ten. The Arab-Israeli War of 1973, however, shattered the status quo and certainly in recent years both the domestic and industrial scene has turned from oil to other fuels. Until recently Government assistance, in the form of Department of Energy grants, was available for converting existing plant to coal-burning.

The transportation of oil is really the transportation of many different types of oil. Crude oil is taken into the refinery and, broadly speaking, black oils and white oils are produced. The former are fuel oils which are used for steam raising and in turn can be light, medium or heavy. At the very bottom, bitumen and petroleum coke are produced. The white oils include kerosene, gas oils like Derv, central heating fuels, gasolenes and even liquefied petroleum gases (LPGs). It is unfortunate that the fuel oils have in recent years shown the greatest decline, since this is the area where rail is strongly placed. The medium and heavy fuel oils must be kept warm during transportation and therefore cannot be sent down a pipeline. Bitumen and heavy fuel oil will even solidify. The white oils, which include the transport fuels, are a growth area, but are in fact, the very oils which can easily be sent down a pipeline.

Nor is pipeline the only competition that British Rail faces. Coastal shipping, barges both coastal and inland, and road vehicles, all have their share. Then there are the exchange agreements between the oil companies, whereby, for example, Company A in the south, needing oil for its outlets in the north, will exchange x-tonnes of oil with Company B in the north, who similarly wants oil for its southern outlets. An excellent way of avoiding transportation costs, but British Rail lose out. Only air transport does not compete!

The major forwarding points in the North East are Lindsey Oil refinery, run by Total Oil and Petrofina, and Humber Oil Refinery, run by Conoco. They are sited next to each other

The Immingham – Kingsbury train has a trailing load of over 1,600 tonnes. Nos 31273 and 31302 run through Melton Ross with the Humber – Kingsbury train on 10th August 1988.

Nos 31185 and 31207 are in charge of empty Total tanks as they pass through Scunthorpe on 7th July 1988, en route to Lindsey from Leeds ORT.

No. 47277 hauls a train of BP tanks through Melton Ross towards Immingham. On-shore crude oil from the BP Welton field at Lincoln is brought to Immingham for further processing.

No. 56089 passes Hartlepool Docks with the Sunderland – Lindsey Petrofina empties on 28th June 1988.

Petroleum coke from Humber Oil Refinery is sent to RTZ at Holyhead on Thursdays only. No. 47223 restarts from Healey Mills after a crew change on 18th August 1988. The black hopper wagons are very distinctive.

at Immingham. There are very heavy flows from Lindsey to Nottingham, Birmingham and the Thames Valley. Indeed the heaviest train from the area leaves Immingham for Kingsbury. In the winter two trains a day run, the 6M35 01.55 (MSX) from Lindsey and the 6M57 09.34 (SX) from Humber. Both are hauled by two Class 31s and have a trailing load of 1,632 tonnes. In the summer this is reduced to one train a day, alternating in the week between the two refineries. The heaviest train running solely within the North East is the 6N95 02.25 (MSX) Lindsey to Sunderland hauled by a Class 56. The trailing load is 1,428 tonnes in 14 railcars. It is interesting that the latter is a movement won from coastal shipping on the basis of price and reliability. Another very heavy train within the North East is the Port Clarence to Leeds which similarly hauls 14 100 tonners. In terms of productivity this train is the more significant since it is Class 47-hauled. Although Shell are nationally Railfreight's biggest customer, within the North East the honour goes to Total. About a million tonnes per annum are moved for Total. From Lindsey, white oils are sent on behalf of Petrofina to terminals as widespread as Colwick, Bedworth, Langley and Sunderland.

The 6M32 03.26 (ThSX) Lindsey to Preston is an interesting working. It is headed by a pair of Class 31s and as well as conveying black and white oils, it also has bitumen on the back in short wheelbase wagons for Landfina. The train is designated a class 6 on the outward run and a class 7 on the return. This is because short wheelbase wagons, unless they have special springs, are allowed to run at 60mph loaded but only at 45mph empty. The return working, 7E60, leaves Preston at 10.40, arriving at 16.24. The 6L42 04.08 (SX) Lindsey to Leeds, is a Total train which can carry black or white oils, the return working being 6D42 08.36 (SX). This working is accomplished with one driver throughout. After booking on, he goes to the refinery and works the train to Leeds. He remains with the train whilst it is being discharged, then works the train back to Lindsey. The last journey is light engine back to the depot where he signs off. There are three such workings in the day from Immingham, the others being the 6L33 12.38 Lindsey - Leeds and the 6L34 14.35 Lindsey - Leeds, both SX. One is for Total, the other for Elf. Some trains, such as those to Kingsbury, Leeds and Sunderland can be of mixed oils. Fuel oil is sent to Skellow, Oakleigh and Brownhills, whilst Colwick also receives black oils. The 7M25 03.56 (TThO) to Ashton-in-Makerfield delivers bitumen, the returns being via the 7E34 11.02. As well as carrying white oils the 6V68 21.23 (SX) Lindsey-Langley also supplies aviation spirit for London Heathrow Airport.

The 6D61 06.38 (TThO) takes fuel oil from Lindsey to Cottam CEGB, but is an infrequent runner. It is diagrammed to show that British Rail has the resources to run it to Cottam or to other power stations if required. Humber Oil sends white oil to Langley, Bedworth, Kingsbury and Glazebrook, and also petroleum coke to Holyhead on the 21.51 (WO), the return working leaving at 07.40 on

No. 47224 backs the Port Clarence (Phillips) to Leeds derv train into the Leeds Oil Rail Terminal on the 1st June 1987.

The 1,008 tonnes of derv will take two hours to unload. The terminal can accommodate 28 TEA 'hundred tonners', 14 on each side.

No. 47085 in new oil sub-sector livery is seen at Colton South Junction on 27th July 1988, heading for Jarrow with the Shell train from Stanlow.

On the 14th December 1987, No. 37147 is ready to depart from Jarrow with the empty BP tanks for Grangemouth.

Appleton Associates at Scarborough receive oil from Stanlow about once every three weeks. No. 47278 negotiates the curves at Kirkham Abbey with the return empties.

No. 47324 enters Skipton on 4th August 1988 with the twice weekly train of bitumen from Stanlow. The bitumen is used in the main by road construction companies.

Thursday. The train is hauled by a Class 47. A glimpse into the future was to be had in March 1988 when British Rail ran a trial with 20 100 tonners on one train hauled by two Class 47s from Lindsey to Colwick. The operation was pronounced a success and when a signal at Grantham has been moved, it is British Rail's intention to introduce the working.

On Teesside two companies, Phillips and ICI, have a joint interest in the refining of oil. ICI's petrol is produced as a by-product from chemical processes. Phillips deal mainly with the burning oils and deliver to Long Eaton, Derby, Bromsgrove, Leeds Oil Rail Terminal and Weaste. ICI has a stock movement from Billingham to British Tar Products at Glazebrook. This train usually runs Tuesday to Saturday and hauls about 600 tonnes of petrol. It is, in fact, the train that caught fire in Summit Tunnel in 1984. On 1st January 1988 ICI sold its petrol interest to Burmah Oil. The petrol movement is therefore now by Burmah's railfleet and is their rail movement.

One of the largest terminals in the North East is the Leeds Oil Rail Terminal (ORT). It has two sidings, each capable of taking 14 100-tonners, and receives about half a million tonnes of product a year. Opened in 1967, the terminal is privately owned. Most week-days it receives four trains — one from Port Clarence (Phillips) and three from Lindsey (Total and Elf) with occasional trains from Stanlow and Humber. Shell have their own rail terminal adjacent to ORT which receives two trains a day from Stanlow (Shell). Although there has been a slight upturn of late in the throughput of fuel oils, the decline in this product is well documented here, there now being only the occasional train a week. Gas oils and petrols are the main fuels handled.

Shell U.K. Oil at Stanlow Refinery send on average eight 1,400 tonnes gross trains per week to the Shell U.K. Oil, Jarrow Distribution Terminal. These are the 6E15 00.19 (TFO), arriving 07.05 and the 6E18 07.55 (SX) arriving 14.03. Product is also sent from the B.P. Oil Refinery at Grangemouth in Scotland on the 6E58 19.56 (TWO) arriving at 05.15. These trains are normally 990 tonnes gross and the oil is stored for BP Oil by Shell U.K. Oil at Jarrow. All grades of petroleum products are handled at Jarrow, trains carrying a combination of fuel oils, gas oils and petroleum.

Appletons Associates of York, Harrogate and Scarborough also receive oil from Stanlow. Arriving in the early morning the train splits at York, where the tanks are forwarded to Harrogate and Scarborough with the occasional five tanks for Foss Island at York. Until 1987 a shunter tripped the oil to the terminal in Scarborough, but since Scarborough lost its pilot, this is now done by the locomotive. Formerly the locomotive returned with the empties, but recent workings show that it now waits for the tanks to be unloaded and returns in the late afternoon (16.10) to pick up the empties in York. Workings are intermittent, Mondays or Wednesdays about every three weeks in the winter, and it must be said that small tonnages such as this must be very susceptible to road competition. The York terminal was the most vulnerable as it is on the end

On 10th January 1988, one of ICI's 640hp Thos Hill 'Steelman' 6-wheel diesel-hydraulic shunters hauls a train of motor spirit from their loading bays into the reception sidings at Billingham. The train will then go forward via Summit Tunnel to Glazebrook.

No. 47299 passes Brocklesby with the Colwick – Lindsey empties on 7th July 1988.

of the line that served Rowntrees. Since the latter no longer use rail, this movement of approximately five tanks is the only justification for keeping the line open. Inevitably a decision has been taken to close the Foss Island branch at the end of 1988.

There is one part of the oil market which was originally regarded as a growth area — on-shore crude. Although the price of crude oil did not increase significantly in the year 1987-88, it is still quite exciting for British Rail since many parts of the country are now under licence for exploration, including some in the North East. Furthermore it is an area where rail can compete as the finds are near railways. The Welton field north of Lincoln sends about 125,000 tonnes of crude into Immingham Storage Company for B.P. by rail each year. The trains are the 7D90 15.14 (MWThO) and the 16.21 (TFO), the workings being completed using only one locomotive.

Colas Roads (Jobling Purser) of Newcastle upon Tyne bring in bitumen by rail from Stanlow Oil Refinery at Ellesmere Port. This is then either distributed by road on behalf of Shell Bitumen U.K. Ltd to their North East customers in the road building and maintenance industry, or it is processed by Colas Roads into various types of emulsions, paints and compounds for use in road maintenance, building or pipeline industries. The annual throughput is about 31,000 tonnes, the peak usage being between the months of June and September when the turnover can be as high as 4,000 to 5,000 tonnes a month. The bitumen is delivered by Speedlink from Stanlow.

Another company which handles bitumen is Croda Hydrocarbons of Kilnhurst near Rotherham. The hot bitumen is delivered from the Mobil Refinery at Coryton by the 6J44 21.21 (MWFO) Ripple Lane to Kilnhurst West, arriving at 05.14. Because the bitumen trade is seasonal, Croda averages one or two trainloads a week during the winter period but this can rise to five or six in the summer.

Stanlow Shell also sends heavy fuel oil and gas oil to Tees Storage Company which has a rail siding at its Middlesbrough storage terminal. This normally arrives by Speedlink in 700 tonne loads. British Rail delivers the railcars onto the Dock Estate and the Tees Storage Company locomotive then collects and takes them to the terminal.

The workhorse of the wagon fleets is the 102 tonne tank wagon, usually referred to as the 'hundred tonner'. With a 25½ tonne axle loading, these wagons can carry up to 75 tonnes of product, depending on their design. There are two types of 102 tonne tanker, Class A and Class B. Class A are for the white oils — petrol, kerosene, Derv, gas oils — any oil which looks clear. These do not need any insulation. The Class B railcars are for fuel oils, the black oils, and since the latter can solidify, the tankers are insulated. Bitumen requires a further category of railcar, one which has not only insulation and heating coils, but also flame tubes to reheat the product should transit times be extended for any reason. The bitumen is loaded hot at the refinery and ideally is transported and unloaded quickly so that it does not need to be reheated. Another type of tanker is the pressure vessel which is needed for the liquid petroleum gases. Although there is no LPG movement in the North East at the time of writing, Humber Oil Refinery is considering marketing it again in the near future. Whether this will come from the storage facility jointly owned with Calor in Killingholme Caverns or whether it will be loaded directly from the

The flame tubes are lit on a bitumen tank wagon at Skipton. The oil is reheated to make it flow more easily for discharge.

production line is not yet known. There is a limit of one tank of LPG per train if there is no guard and neither LPG nor petrol will be allowed through the Channel Tunnel.

All railcars are either owned by the oil companies or are hired. Some are coming to the end of their working lives and are being replaced by the companies. There has also been considerable intermediate building. Esso did experiment with an aluminium railcar but the idea failed to take off. That there was less tare weight seemed an attractive proposition but problems arose with the integrity of the welds.

In general the real costs of distribution in this country are declining for all types of transport. Such innovations as driver-only operation have enabled British Rail to cut its costs and to improve its financial performance against government targets. Even greater productivity benefits should accrue when the Class 60 locomotives are available. Less maintenance costs and longer trains, for example. The Class 47 has been the archetypal oil train locomotive for the best part of 30 years now and prices to customers have always been based on what a Class 47 can haul. However, there is now a move away from this pricing policy and the North East petroleum sub-sector has only ten Class 47s but fourteen Class 31s! On average the Class 47 will pull 1,020 tonnes, that is ten 102 tonne tanks. Yet on some routes they can do better. From Lindsey to the Thames Valley they can lift 15 because the gradients happen to be favourable. A Class 56 can improve marginally on this, 14 on a Class 47 translating into 16 or 17 railcars. What is noteworthy, however, is that the load for a Class 47 from Grangemouth to Aberdeen is seven 102 tonners. Yet a locomotive with the adhesion capability of a Class 59, and presumably a Class 60, could haul 24 over the same route. The mind boggles!

The corollary of this agreement seems simple. A Class 60 would give such enormous productivity benefits in terms of haulage that costs would drop dramatically both for British Rail and the customer. But it is not as simple as that. The demand in Scotland or anywhere else may not be great enough for such loads and existing terminals could not handle that length of train. We have seen that the largest in the North East can take 14 tankers on each side. Many, including the new Petrofina terminal at Sunderland, can handle only seven on each side. A way around this might be to run mixed company trains, 14 tanks each from Lindsey and Humber. Half the train could be dropped off at one terminal the rest going on to the second. This would mean time spent shunting the train in and putting it together again afterwards. Even so, it would be financially advantageous to both companies. The reason this has not happened to date, even with lower haulage capacity is due to the conservative attitude of the oil companies themselves. They may well want to refine their economics, but the marketing men, who wish to keep their territory secret and their rivals out, have so far won the day. Certainly, in dealing with different companies, manageability and flexibility would suffer and probably reliability too. Company A might cancel its half, leaving British Rail with half a train. If the inherent problems could be ironed out however, the mixed train would appear to hold considerable advantages for the future.

The 6L34 Lindsey – Leeds is for the Elf Petrol Company. No. 47295 passes Thorne Junction heading for Leeds on 18th August 1988.

Chapter 4

Metals and Automotive

The railways have always been involved in the movement of metals traffic, from the raw materials to the carrying of steel to the ports for export. Up to 1967 there were numerous large and small private iron and steel companies with their own ore mines and limestone quarries. The traffic then was often wagonload rather than trainload, with flows criss-crossing the country in a most haphazard manner.

In July 1967 the British Steel Corporation was formed from the larger steel companies, although most of the semi-finishing and specialist producers were left private. The aim of the BSC was to get rid of the large number of small outdated works and introduce new modern competitive plants. Steelmaking was to be centred on five areas: Scunthorpe, Sheffield, Teesside, South Wales and Scotland.

Because of their poor iron yield, home-produced ores were proving expensive. Imported ores had on average a 62% iron content compared with 27% from British ores. A decision was therefore taken that it would be cheaper to use imported ore in the long term. Today the main steel producing centres in the North East are at Sheffield, Scunthorpe and Teesside, the last two being well situated for deep water ports where the vast tonnages of iron ore have to be landed.

Similarly, the British Steel blast furnaces are on or near the coast. Redcar, which has the largest blast furnace in Europe, receives its iron ore direct from the ship. Scunthorpe, whose four blast furnaces are known throughout the world as the 'Four Queens' — Anne, Victoria, Mary and Bess — bring their iron ore into the Immingham ore terminal as 'fines'. This fine ore comes from Venezuela, Brazil and Canada. Also from Canada, and from Norway, come the half inch round ore pellets. About four million tonnes of imported ore pass through Immingham every year.

The ore is moved from the ship to the stocking area by conveyor belt. At the railhead it is stored in three 1,000 tonne overhead bunkers. Three 100 tonne PTA wagons can be loaded simultaneously, each receiving a measured 75 tonnes of ore. The Scunthorpe operation requires five sets of 21 wagons: one on maintenance, one on stand-by, and three sets working. The trains operate with a trailing load of 2,100 tonnes.

The wagons, owned by British Steel, have an 'A' end and a 'B' end. A fixed type of buckeye coupling is fitted at one end and the other has a rotary buckeye coupling. The wagons are coupled 'A' to 'B' in the train, only the two outer wagons being fitted with conventional couplings and buffers.

From Monday to Friday sixteen trains a day and on Saturday ten trains a day move the ore to Santon, Scunthorpe. The wagons are tippled individually to discharge the ore and, thanks to the rotary couplings, the train does not have to uncouple. The trains are hauled by pairs of Class 37 locomotives from Immingham which now have double fuel tanks fitted. They remain away from their shed for 48 hours, being refuelled on Wednesdays and Sundays only!

Coke is necessary to the steelmaking process. To produce the coke, about 31,000 tonnes of coal are delivered to Scunthorpe each week from various collieries. The coal is of a low sulphur type and is delivered in the usual 1,000 tonne

trainloads. Not all the coke required by Scunthorpe is produced on site. The British Steel coking ovens at Orgreave, Sheffield, produce some 5,500 tonnes each week which is sent to Scunthorpe in HEAs.

Limestone is also needed for the process. As described in the Minerals chapter, flows for the steelworks on Teesside originate at Redmire and the British Steel-owned Hardendale Quarry at Shap in Cumbria. Scunthorpe and Sheffield, however, receive their limestone, which is quarried locally, by road.

The iron ore, coke and limestone are mixed together in the blast furnace to produce molten iron. This has still to be converted into steel and can be done in different ways. Both Scunthorpe and Teesside use the basic oxygen process. The molten iron is moved in huge 320 tonne capacity torpedo ladle rail wagons from the blast furnace to the steel-producing vessels using British Steel's internal railway system. It is poured into the vessels and selected grades of scrap metal are added. An oxygen lance then blows pure oxygen into the charge to remove any impurities. Normally piped from the plant, the oxygen can, however, be delivered during maintenance periods in British Oxygen Company's own 100 tonne bogie cryogenic tank wagons. At Scunthorpe and on Teesside they are taken to local Railfreight terminals where the liquid oxygen is transferred to road tanker. Because of the thickness of the metal, the rail

Nos 37010 and 37106 haul an iron ore train through the loading bunker at Immingham on 16th April 1987. Three wagons are filled simultaneously with a measured 75 tonnes of ore.

Pairs of Class 37s shuttle the iron ore from Immingham to Scunthorpe. Nos 37225 and 37042 approach Brocklesby with empty wagons on 7th July 1988.

A rotary buckeye coupling. The couplings rotate about each other enabling individual wagons to be completely inverted without uncoupling the train.

Dolofines for British Steel at Ravenscraig move daily from Steetley's Thrislington Quarry at Ferryhill. No. 37092 passes through Columbia on the Leamside line on 23rd August 1988.

Molten iron is moved in these giant torpedo ladles. A British Steel 6-wheel diesel electric shunter, No.269 Longacres (GEC 5466 of 1977) hauls two empties from Lackenby to Redcar.

No. 47301 negotiates the cliff tops at Hunt Cliff with the 9P61 trip from Skinningrove on 26th August 1988. The train includes scrap metal in MDW wagons for Lackenby.

Nos 20113 and 20061 depart from the UES site at Aldwarke with empty POA scrap wagons for Tinsley Yard.

tankers carry only 50 tonnes of oxygen. The rail system serving the steel centres with oxygen is an integrated network involving all BOC plants around the country.

At British Steel Scunthorpe the necessary scrap metal is obtained both internally and locally and no Railfreight movements are involved. On Teesside, however, it is obtained from rail-connected scrap merchants in the Tyneside, Wearside and Hartlepool areas and from British Steel's special profile mills at Skinningrove on the coast nearby. The scrap is transported to Lackenby in vacuum-braked, air-piped MDW 21 tonne flat-bottom ex-coal wagons. Also on Teesside the British Steel 20in pipe mill at Hartlepool moves scrap metal in air-braked HSA wagons to the pipe mill at Clydesdale in Scotland on Speedlink workings. These wagons are surplus HEA coal hoppers with the bottom discharge floor welded up.

A further major steelmaking process is the electric arc furnace method. This method allows a far greater control over the quality of the metal and is to be found mainly in Sheffield, an area noted for its fine quality steels. The process uses large quantities of cold steel scrap. Carbon electrodes are lowered into the furnace, an arc is struck and the heat generated melts the scrap. The quantities required cannot be obtained locally and are brought into Sheffield by rail. Most of it moves under what is known as the Standard Railfreight Scrap Scheme.

In 1984 a scheme involving Standard Railfreight, British Rail and United Engineering Steels (UES) at Sheffield was evolved whereby scrap is collected by Railfreight from rail-connected scrap merchants from as far afield as Workington and London. It is loaded into the distinctive blue and yellow 51 tonne POA wagons and Railfreight delivers the wagons to UES who have a certain time to discharge them before Railfreight collects and returns them to the merchants' yards. The aim of the scheme is to make best use of the wagons. The whole circuit should take no longer than five days to complete. If one of the parties cannot meet his commitment, he incurs a penalty for delay. The wagons complete the trunk haul at night on Speedlink. In this way 375,000 tonnes of scrap a year are transported by rail. The UES sites are at Aldwarke in Rotherham and Stocksbridge, north west of Sheffield, Tinsley Yard being the focal point for the POA wagons. UES also receives two trainloads a week from the Ford Motor Company at Halewood on Merseyside, and there are flows of scrap metal out of Sheffield and the North East to Sheerness Steels, a private company in Kent. The scrap is in Procor-built 100 tonne bogie scrap wagons, some with the Sheerness Steel name on the side.

When we say that Railfreight carries steel, the statement should perhaps be qualified. Railfreight carries many types of steel. Most seen on rail comes under the heading of semi-finished steel: finished steel is not as common, accounting for only a small proportion of steel moved by Railfreight. A description at this point of semi-finished steels might help the reader to recognise what is being carried.

A **billet** is a long thin piece of metal approximately 6in square which can be rolled flat, drawn into wire, made into small sections or drop-forged into engine crank cases. The main flow of billet in the North East is two, sometimes three,

900 tonne trains with twelve BFA bogie bolsters every day from British Steel at Scunthorpe to Railfreight's Masborough Steel Terminal at Rotherham. The wagons have raised bolsters to allow the Hermes fork lift truck to unload the billet and place it on road vehicles for the final delivery to the nearby Templeborough rolling mills. There are also flows from Scunthorpe to the West Midlands, the Cardiff rod mill and even one to Northern Italy by train ferry.

UES send billet from their Aldwarke Works to GKN at Cardiff and to various rolling mills in the Black Country. There is also a flow of concast billet across Rotherham on BCW wagons from the UES Templeborough mini-plant to the Thrybergh bar and 11in mills at Aldwarke. It is also despatched to east coast ports for export to the EEC.

Blooms are large blocks of metal about 400mm thick and up to 7 metres long. They are moved by rail from the basic steelmaking centres to the other mills for further processing. Significant flows are from Lackenby to the British Steel rail mill at Workington: to British Steel at Shelton for their beam and section mills: and from Lackenby to the special profiles division at Skinningrove. They are usually carried on BBA wagons.

Slabs are about 200mm thick and up to 9 metres long. They are moved to hot rolling mills where they are processed into plates or coils. At Sheffield British Steel Stainless have two rail-connected complexes separated by Tinsley Yard. Stainless steel slabs move by rail on BDA or SPA wagons from the stainless melting and continuous casting site (SMACC) to either Port Talbot or Lackenby for rolling, before returning to their Shepcote Lane site some 400 yards away.

Another important flow for Railfreight is from the SMACC site to the east coast ports of Grimsby and Goole. The slabs are shipped to Europe for specialist rolling before returning via the east coast ports. Railfreight completes the haul back to Sheffield. In addition, approximately 5,000 tonnes of slabs are moved each week on BAA and BBA wagons between the British Steel works of Scunthorpe and Lackenby.

High quality **wire rod in coil** is produced by Scunthorpe rod mill for the UK and export markets. A high percentage of their production is carried by Railfreight. Regular traffic flows for the home market are to Sheffield, South Wales, the Midlands and Stoke. These amount to 76,000 tonnes a year, with a further 56,000 tonnes passing through northern ports for export. The coils are carried on SKA, SPA, BPA or SRV wagons and are always sheeted. The flow to Stoke via Longport is carried in VTG-owned ferry wagons which have the Scunthorpe rod mill logo and name on the side. The wire rods are further processed and used for making wire ropes, springs, barbed wire, tyre bead and cords, and pins and needles. The UES 11in mill at Aldwarke also despatches wire coil by rail to Immingham and Flixborough Wharf for export, mainly to the USA, and the UES Thrybergh bar mill moves 1/2in to 11/2in bars on BCW and SPA wagons to the Midlands.

Hot rolled plate coil is produced at Lackenby and is mainly used in pipe making. Two trains a day leave

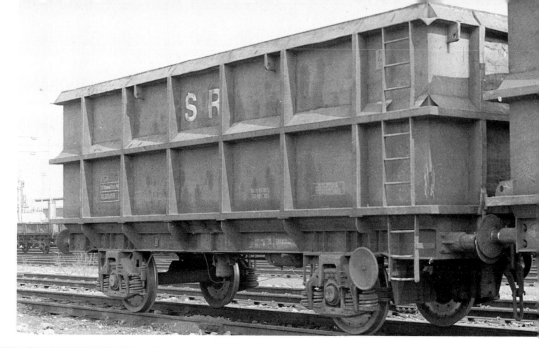

One hundred and eighty one of these 51 tonne POA scrap wagons operate on the Standard Railfreight Scrap Scheme.

One of the Hermes fork lift trucks unloads billet from a BFA raised bolster wagon at Rotherham Masborough Steel Terminal. The billet arrives daily from Scunthorpe.

On the 11th January 1988, No. 37507 Hartlepool Pipe Mill passes Shepherds House with the Lackenby to Skinningrove bloom train.

Billets are long thin bars of metal. No. 37255 passes the Thomas Hill locomotive works at Kilnhurst with the morning Scunthorpe - Rotherham billet train on 14th July 1988.

No. 37258 passes Kirk Sandall on 22nd August 1988 with stainless steel slabs from the S.M.A.C.C. site at Sheffield bound for Europe via Grimsby for specialist rolling.

The stainless steel slabs return to this country as rolled coil. No. 37106 enters Scunthorpe Yard on 10th August 1988 with a train of coil from Grimsby Docks.

Lackenby for the British Steel pipe mill at Corby, Northants. The coil is positioned on the BAAs 'on the roll'. It is hot and the decks of the wagons have gaps for air to flow through to cool the coils. They may have a rusty appearance but this is a protective rust. The trailing weight of the trains is 2,100 tonnes and they are always hauled by a pair of dedicated Class 37s from Thornaby depot. There is also a daily train of hot rolled plate coil from Lackenby to the British Steel 20in pipe mill at Hartlepool. The coil is laid 'eye to sky', that is, standing on end. The reason for this is that at Hartlepool the coil is unloaded by tongs, whilst the Lackenby-Corby traffic is unloaded by a gantry crane with a 'C' hook. Lackenby also produce 'Durbar' flooring with a non-slip pattern — the type used on ships' decking and other walkways — and this moves by rail in plate coils.

Plate is moved either in trainload or on Speedlink from Scunthorpe to the 44in pipe mill at Hartlepool for large diameter pipe making. When the ship-building industries on the Tyne and Wear win new orders, plate moves from Scunthorpe to the area.

Pipes are produced at the 44in and 20in pipe mills at Hartlepool and are moved in 21 wagon train loads to Leith in Scotland. They move on BQW bogie bolster wagons fitted with wooden saddles to accommodate the various size pipes. At Leith the pipes are coated with concrete or bitumen and will be used in the oil and gas pipeline industry. Before being moved again the saddles have to be changed because of the increased pipe diameter. British Tubes Stockholding Ltd at Stourton, Leeds, receive various sizes of pipe mainly from Corby and the 20in mill at Hartlepool. This traffic is Speedlink and is tripped from Hunslet into the company sidings. Another semi-finished product is reinforcing bar for the construction industry. This comes from South Wales to Sheffield Freight Terminal.

In the finished steels sector, the special profiles works at Skinningrove produce 'bulb flats' which form part of the framing for ships. These are moved by rail as and when required to ship-building areas both in this country and abroad. The same works exports Grouser track shoes for caterpillar-tracked vehicles to West Germany and Italy. Fish plates are also made at Skinningrove, whilst the rails are produced at Workington and are moved to Teesside for export.

As can be seen, numerous steel items travel by rail; some are long-term contracts, others come and go almost overnight. British Steel's contract to supply Larssen steel piling for the Channel Tunnel was one which Railfreight was well placed to win because of the tonnages and distance involved. Trainloads of piling moved on BDA and BDW wagons daily until the contract finished some six months after it began. At present, British Steel are supplying constructional steel for the Tunnel.

Scunthorpe Rod Mill uses these VTG wagons to move wire rod to Stoke for use in the manufacture of motor vehicle tyres.

Sheffield Freight Terminal is a busy yard. Overhead gantry cranes are used to handle the larger objects. Here a Jones mobile crane lifts wire coil from an SPA wagon.

Stockholders, processors and warehousing

Throughout the North East there are a number of rail-connected steel stockholders and companies which provide warehousing and distribution services. In the Leeds area, Dunlop Ranken at Farnley are one such company. A daily trip from Hunslet Yard conveys steel sections. The steel originates from Teesside, Scunthorpe and Shelton, some 25,000 tonnes being received annually at the company's private sidings. Final delivery is by road because of the small quantities involved and road's speed of delivery for short journeys.

D&F Steels at Stourton are stockholders, fabricators and distributors. They receive about 30,000 tonnes of light and heavy sections a year, mainly from Scunthorpe, though some steel is imported from the Continent.

Other steel stockholders in the Leeds area who are not rail-connected, rely on the facilities at Leeds Whitehall Road goods depot or Cobra's Railfreight Terminal at Wakefield. The latter receive large quantities of steel in various forms from the major producers and from the continent via a daily trip from Doncaster Belmont Yard. Cobra unload the steel and deliver it to the stockholders by road.

In the Middlesbrough area, road haulier A.V. Dawson has sidings at Cargo Fleet where various steel products are taken in and distributed. Nearby, Stockton Haulage Ltd are a rail-connected haulage company with storage facilities. They also have other depots at Holyhead and Stranraer, the latter depot being the first Section 8 grant awarded in the country. The company has a daily trip conveying a whole range of steel products. These include sections, pipes, coiled sheet, blooms, slabs and rails. They use both rail and road to deliver the steel to the home market or to local ports for export. They also serve their Stranraer depot with steel bound for Ireland.

Cleveland Bridge and Engineering Ltd of Darlington are steel constructional engineers with rail sidings. They take in various sizes of beams, plate and sections, though none of the finished products moves out by rail.

These SKA coil carrying wagons can carry 31 tonnes of coil. No. 460846 is seen at Sheffield Freight Terminal fully laden. The coil is stacked in two rows along a cradle.

Coil is off-loaded onto BRS owned road vehicles which are on contract to Railfreight and painted in their colours. The coils are taken by road to customers who are not rail connected.

Hot rolled plate coil fits on the BAA wagons in cradles. Two Thornaby metals sub-sector Class 37s head the 6M47 Lackenby to Corby 2,100 tonne train through South Bank. No. 37502 leads No. 37511 on 11th March 1987.

Nos 37519 and 37504 head south at Colton with the 6M47 Lackenby-Corby train on 23rd June 1988.

This lovely-looking, and practical wagon is a VTG owned 88 tonne Ferrywagon. It has telescopic hoods for easy loading and is used to transport all types of steel, particularly those vulnerable to the elements.

New liveried No. 37521 passes South Bank on 15th August 1988 with steel coil ('eye to sky') for the 20 inch pipe mill at Hartlepool.

These BQW bogie wagons are the perfect size for transporting 12 metre pipe from the Hartlepool pipe mill. The wooden saddles allow the pipes to be stacked on top of each other.

In the Humberside area, Smallers have sidings at Immingham. They deal in the warehousing and distribution of various steel products. Nearby, Immingham Railfreight Terminals Ltd have large rail-connected storage sheds. They tend to store steel in the form of wire coils or sections until such times as a ship berths. The steel is then forwarded to the docks for export.

The main rail-connected export terminals within the North East are the Humber ports of Grimsby, Immingham, Goole and Hull. On Teesside is Tees Dock, which in 1987 exported 1.1 million tonnes of steel. There are also new terminals at Seaham and Sunderland. Exports consist of anything from rails for Commonwealth countries to slabs for the USA. Slightly more steel is exported than imported, Railfreight usually moving the steel forward from the works to the docks. Imports tend to be mixed batches of steel products and a daily working from Grimsby to Wolverhampton conveys the imports. Some steels which are vulnerable to the elements are imported via the train ferries at Dover. These move in Transfesa, VTG or Cargowaggon ferry vehicles, making their way north on Speedlink.

The prospects for export via the Channel Tunnel look good for the Metals sub-sector in the North. The distances travelled will be favourable to rail and there are many private rail sidings in Europe. The Tunnel is unlikely to affect steel movements to Northern Europe since it is unlikely to be economic to send a train from Teesside through the Tunnel to head back north again. This traffic is likely to continue with shipping. However, for companies wishing to export to Europe, there could well be direct trains from, say, Scunthorpe — with feeder services from Teesside, Sheffield and other areas — to Amiens to service Northern France and Paris; or Scunthorpe to Basel, serving Northern Italy, Switzerland, Austria and Southern Germany.

In November 1986 an experiment began at Thornaby. All Metals trains were identified, re-diagrammed and a fleet of locomotives identified against each diagram. Only the allocated locomotives would work these diagrams and they would be maintained solely at Thornaby depot. This practice was criticised initially, since if the pair of Class 37/5 locomotives on the Lackenby-Corby failed at Chesterfield,

two more locomotives dedicated to the Metals traffic would have to travel light engine to Chesterfield to continue the train. The former practice was to remove a locomotive from any convenient train. The system has been modified and is now more flexible, different sectors and sub-sectors borrowing spare capacity locomotives as and when required. Dedication has certainly benefited the Metals sub-sector and has led to locomotive availability being improved to the point where weekly figures of 90% availability are not uncommon. This means that more trains can run with the same number of locomotives — and reliability enhances customer confidence.

The Metals sub-sector in the North East will receive early allocations of the Class 60 heavy freight locomotive and it is anticipated that one Class 60 will replace two Class 37s. The total allocation of Metals sub-sector locomotives in the North East are:

Thornaby
4 Class 20
6 Class 37/0
2 Class 47
20 Class 37/5
Immingham
20 Class 20
11 Class 37/0
Total: 63 locomotives

The two Class 47 locomotives at Thornaby are short-term planning locomotives, catering for the commencement of new traffics.

Plant shut-downs, works holidays and planned maintenance lead to Railfreight running many special Metals sub-sector trains. For instance, because British Steel plants support each other, slabs, blooms, billets etc may move from one plant to another. New orders are gained and some contracts expire, therefore a list of the working of steel traffic can only be a guide. The following workings may vary and those listed as empties may convey steel returning to a particular area.

No. 37510 passes Cowpen Bewley on 28th June 1988 with a pipe train from Hartlepool to Leith in Scotland.

Main Line Loaded Metals Trains

6N64	Alcan Lynemouth to Tees	Aluminium slabs (Freightliner flats)
6S66	Blyth to Fort William	Alumina
6E47	Cardiff to Tees	Coil ex Port Talbot, slabs ex Sheffield
6M71	Grimsby to Wolverhampton	Imported steel
6M47	Lackenby to Corby	Steel plate coils
6M29	Lackenby to Corby	Steel plate coils
6M78	Lackenby to Shelton	Blooms and other Shelton traffic
6M71	Lackenby to Workington	Blooms for rail mill
6J25	Scunthorpe to Masborough or Aldwarke, Sheffield FT or Templeborough	Billet or rod
6M51	Scunthorpe to Brierley Hill	General steel for West Midlands
6V58	Scunthorpe to Cardiff	Billet and rod
6J55	Scunthorpe to Masborough	Billet
6J57	Scunthorpe to Masborough	Billet
6M59	Scunthorpe to Wolverhampton	General steel for West Midlands
6V67	Tees to Cardiff	Aluminium and coil
8N92	Tyne to Tees	Scrap in MDW wagons

Balanced trains – can travel full or empty in any direction

6M13	Scunthorpe to Longport	Rod for Stoke, empties for Longport
6E66	Longport to Scunthorpe	Exports, empty rod wagons
6N87	Scunthorpe to Tees	Export steel, slabs or anything
6N47	Scunthorpe to Tees	Export steel, slabs or anything
6D45	Tees to Scunthorpe	Export steel for Immingham, anything
6D47	Tees to Scunthorpe	Export steel for Immingham, anything

Main Line Empty Metals Trains

6E29	Brierley Hill to Scunthorpe	4E35*	Shelton to Lackenby
6E44	Cardiff to Scunthorpe	6N65	Tees to Lynemouth
6E40	Corby to Lackenby	6D75	Tees to Scunthorpe
6E37	Corby to Lackenby	8N91	Tees to Tyne
6D49	Masborough to Scunthorpe	4E30*	Workington to Lackenby
6D50	Masborough to Scunthorpe	6E96	Wolverhampton to Grimsby
6E46	Mossend to Blyth Dock	6E52	Wolverhampton to Scunthorpe
6D70	Sheffield Freight Terminal to Scunthorpe	* Class 4 (75mph) trains.

On 22nd June 1987, No. 31264 reverses steel sections into the Dunlop Ranken complex at Farnley, Leeds.

D&F Steels at Stourton, Leeds are served by a daily trip from Hunslet Yard. No. 47014 passes the British Tubes stock-holding sidings as it reverses into D&F Steels on 22nd June 1987.

No. 56123 trips the empty Fort William wagons from the reception sidings to the Alcan ship unloading terminal at Blyth. New wagons have been purchased by Alcan for this traffic.

No. 56123 waits to leave the British Alcan ship unloading terminal at Blyth with alumina for Lynemouth on 22nd May 1987.

Aluminium ingots are loaded onto Freightliner flats at Alcan's Lynemouth smelter for movement to Rogerstone in South Wales. The wagons move to Tees Yard where they form the 6V67 metals sub-sector train to Cardiff.

Saab cars are unloaded at Immingham Railfreight Terminal. The cars travel overnight on Speedlink from Harwich as and when demand warrants it. Saab now use the nearby Smallers sidings for unloading.

Aluminium

Also coming under the Metals banner is the movement of materials connected with the production of aluminium. British Alcan, a company with smelters at Lochaber, Fort William and Kinlochleven in Scotland, also have one at Lynemouth. The raw material needed for the process is alumina, a fine white powder which is shipped into the port of Blyth from Jamaica, Africa and Ireland. The Irish alumina is moved by Railfreight from British Alcan's import terminal at Blyth to Lynemouth in trains of 18 45 tonne hopper wagons. These are grey and can carry 32 tonnes of alumina. They are owned by British Alcan. Each year approximately 250,000 tonnes move between Blyth and Lynemouth.

Each weekday a trainload of alumina from Africa and Jamaica is sent from Blyth to Fort William. Usually hauled by a Class 37, the train carries around 400 tonnes. In 1987 the quantity moved was about 100,000 tonnes. Also in 1987, British Alcan secured a Section 8 grant for improvements to the sidings at Fort William and for the purchase of new wagons. Forty three wagons, each capable of carrying 33 tonnes of alumina, have already been delivered.

British Alcan move ingots of aluminium on Freightliner flats from Lynemouth to Rogerstone in South Wales. When the Freightliner terminal closed at Follingsby (Newcastle) British Alcan were faced with a problem of getting the aluminium to Rogerstone. The Rogerstone plant was not rail connected — hence the Freightliner flow. The problem was solved with a five-set Freightliner train moving the aluminium to Tees Yard every day. This train then forms the 6V67 Tees to Cardiff Metals sub sector sponsored train with Freightliner completing the final haul by road. The train from Lynemouth often conveys ferry wagons laden with aluminium for the Continent.

Automotive

In the North East the automotive traffic is nearly all in finished cars and commercial vehicles going for export or as imported vehicles coming from the ports.

Saab import their vehicles at Harwich and move them by rail on autics and cartic fours (PJA) — that is, on four-set articulated car carriers with two decks — to rail-connected sidings at Immingham. Here they are unloaded near to their delivery compound. Ford move cars and light vans daily on Procar 80's cartic fours and car flats from Southampton, Harwich or Dagenham to Toleman's delivery compound at Wrenthorpe, Wakefield.

In 1987 the Dutch trucking company DAF bought out the British Leyland truck business at Leyland in Lancashire. Trucks are still built in Lancashire and are exported to Holland in a semi-finished condition via the roll-on roll-off ferries at Immingham. A twice-weekly train of PKA three-axle comtics conveys DAF trucks from the plant at Leyland to Immingham Docks on Speedlink services. The comtic wagons are operated by MAT-Transauto. In 1988 the Renault car deliveries from Goole to Aberdeen and Stranraer on Speedlink terminated.

Various ports along the east coast have been used for the import of cars with Railfreight picking up some of the dock-to-distribution centre hauls. Traffic carried in or out of the North East is seasonal, ports like Hartlepool gathering up imports when the demand for new registration cars grows. A fair amount of automotive traffic passes through the area, mainly at night. The timetables of these trains are somewhat flexible in order to avoid the increasing thefts and vandalism that this type of train has come to attract.

No. 47194 approaches South Milford with the 4M77 Bathgate to Washwood Heath empty car carrying wagons on 1st June 1987, a train which runs through the area each afternoon/evening except Mondays.

On 16th April 1987, No. 37203 enters Immingham Dock reception sidings with Leyland-DAF trucks for export to Holland. This train originates at the truck plant at Leyland, Lancashire.

A cartic four car carrying set. Each set comprises four wagons permanently coupled together. Note the anti-vandal wire mesh screens.

Chapter 5
Minerals

Mineral trains are some of the heaviest on the British Rail network. Well known are the limestone movements from the Foster Yeoman quarries in Somerset which can produce trains in excess of 4,000 tonnes. The North East cannot compete with loads of this size, but the trains do at least ensure the continued life of some of the branch lines. A good example of this is the Redmire branch whose operation we shall look at later. The line runs from Northallerton, through Bedale to Redmire in Wensleydale and carries limestone to British Steel at Redcar. But for this traffic, it would have closed long ago.

The north eastern area of England has the Pennines and Yorkshire Dales in the west and the moors and wolds in the east. The extraction of minerals from quarries and mines within the National Park boundaries raises environmentally sensitive questions as to how the minerals should be transported out of these areas. Naturally, the Park's Authority does not want fleets of heavy vehicles on roads not designed to take them and it is here that Railfreight has the advantage over road transport. The 1,200 tonnes of limestone carried each weekday by one train from Redmire would require some 90 38 tonne goods vehicle movements — 45 in each direction. The rail movements — one in each direction — scarcely interrupt rural life.

Situated a few miles along the coast road north of Whitby is Boulby Mine. Owned by Cleveland Potash Ltd, it is the only potash mine in Britain. Its shaft penetrates to a depth of 3,500 feet and the seams reach out beneath the North Sea. Its coastal position makes it ideal for sending potash for export and this is done by Railfreight hauling ten large 93 tonne bogie hopper wagons to the nearby export terminal at Tees Dock, Middlesbrough. Each week 12,000 tonnes of potash are moved out in this manner. The hopper wagons, hired from CAIB, are top loading and bottom discharge. They are painted in the company livery of green with white lettering and are known locally as 'Jolly Green Giants'. The salt content of the potash has, by now, however, turned many of the 34 PBA wagons a rusty brown colour. Care is needed in the transportation of potash, for as the mineral is hygroscopic, that is, it attracts moisture, lids have to be fitted to prevent it getting wet. Were it to do so, the potash would solidify, making bottom discharge difficult. Potash is

Nos 37516 and 37515 near Harmby on the 26th July 1988 with the daily Redmire-Redcar limestone train. Slow speed fitted 37/5s have recently been tried on this train.

A 93 tonne PBA bogie hopper wagon operated by Cleveland Potash Ltd. These wagons are known locally as 'Jolly Green Giants'. They convey potash from Boulby to either Teesdock or to Middlesbrough goods terminal.

At Boulby, salt is loaded into the Cobra containers directly from conveyors, whilst potash is loaded via the overhead bunker.

used almost exclusively in the manufacture of fertilisers and is shipped from Teesbulk Handling Terminal at Tees Dock to Malaya, Brazil, Scandinavia and numerous EEC countries.

Potash also moves by rail to various parts of Britain. One movement is in CBA hopper wagons to Papworth's storage depot at Ely. This goes on Speedlink. Another flow is to ICI at Severnside. In this instance, the potash is loaded into containers hired from Cobra Railfreight of Wakefield who also have a depot at Severnside. The containerised potash, with lids, is despatched on Standard Wagon PFA bogie flats from Boulby, then via Speedlink from Tees Yard to Severnside where it is again used in fertiliser production. Potash in granulated form is also moved from Boulby to Middlesbrough Goods in 'Jolly Green Giants'. Here it is put onto road vehicles for delivery to customers without rail access.

As well as potash, rock salt is extracted from an adjacent seam at Boulby. Since Cleveland Potash made the salt

available as a de-icing agent for roads in 1981, it has proved a lucrative business. Significant amounts of around 300,000 to 400,000 tonnes a year are supplied to local authorities. The Cobra containers, without lids, are moved to the Cobra Railfreight depot within the Middlesbrough Goods terminal. They move in 500 tonne trainloads on FEW or PFA wagons and are built with fork pockets in the base to facilitate handling by fork lift trucks.

On arrival at the Cobra terminal, the containers are lifted from the flat wagons by a 25 tonne Lansing fork lift which places them onto a semi-trailer road vehicle. The latter then moves the salt to the stockpile, where the end doors of the containers are opened and the wagon tips its salt. The empty container is placed back on the rail vehicle and the next container is unloaded. A hydraulic excavator loads the salt into lorries for outbase delivery.

Every day about eight trains of potash and rock salt run to Middlesbrough, motive power being provided by Class 20

Some of the potash is exported at Teesdock. A 'Jolly Green Giant' deposits its load which then runs along conveyors to waiting ships.

Nos 37512 and 37506 at Tees Yard on 10th February 1987 with a potash train from Boulby. These wagons will go forward on a Speedlink working to Cobra Railfreight's depot at Severnside for ICI. Note the lids on the wagons to stop the potash becoming wet.

Rock salt used for de-icing roads, is moved from Boulby to Cobra Railfreight depot at Middlesbrough. No. 37693 hauls a train of FEW wagons laden with salt towards Middlesbrough at Skelton, on 31st October 1986.

On arrival at Cobra Railfreight, the salt containers are lifted from the FEW wagons by a Lansing fork lift truck.

The forks engage in pockets and the containers are placed on a road vehicle semi-trailer.

locomotives working in pairs. The five miles of single track line from Boulby to Skinningrove is owned by Cleveland Potash.

At Swinden, between Skipton and Grassington, Tilcon own a large limestone quarry. After blasting, the stone is crushed and graded before being top loaded from a conveyor into a fleet of Tilcon's own PGA hopper wagons. There are 33 of these, painted in the company livery of Wedgewood blue and crimson, with the company name and logo on the side. The wagons serve two Tilcon railheads at Marsh Lane, Leeds and Hull Dairycoates.

Tilcon's Hull terminal, situated next to Dairycoates Yard, receives a daily train of 1,100 tonnes of limestone aggregate which is bottom discharged and fed by conveyor into the company's bitumen macadam plant. Here the stone is mixed with bitumen and used for road surfacing. It is also used as concrete aggregate and building stone, the larger stone being transported according to demand. One train a week, usually a Saturday departure, leaves Swinden for Marsh Lane. Again unloaded by bottom discharge, the stone is used in the making of concrete and marketed as Tilcon Trumix. The traffic generated is considerable, 300,000 tonnes being moved out of the quarry each year. The scenic line from Swinden to Skipton is single track and only Tilcon trains use it. These are always hauled by a pair of Class 31 locomotives.

The end doors on the containers are opened and the salt is tipped onto the stockpile. The container is then placed back on the train.

Not too far away at Redmire in Wensleydale, Tarmac own a quarry which is operated by British Steel. The limestone quarried here is used as a flux in the iron-making process at Redcar on Teesside which consumes some 6,000 tonnes a week. As the quarry is not directly linked by rail, road vehicles bring the stone from the quarry to the railhead, a distance of about a mile. The lorries reverse up a ramp to the bunker and tip the stone which is then fed into the rail wagons. The top loading, bottom discharge PGA hoppers are owned by British Steel and are grey with the company

Continued Page 62

The line from Middlesbrough to Boulby passes very close to the cliff edge at Hunt Cliff. Nos 20156 and 20144 lead a train of empty potash and salt wagons towards Boulby on the 26th August 1988.

Tilcon at Swinden Quarry employ two ex BR diesel electric shunters to work their yard. No. 08054 is seen at the quarry on 10th March 1987.

Nos 31206 and 31126 haul the daily 1,100 tonnes of limestone bound for Hull on 10th March 1987 at Clints Rock, Rylstone.

The limestone is discharged at Hull Dairycoates by pneumatically operated bottom doors onto a conveyor belt.

The hopper wagons are loaded with limestone at Redmire from road vehicles, via an overhead bunker.

Nos 20070 Leyburn *and 20173* Wensleydale *prepare the daily 1,700 tonne trailing weight train of limestone under the shadow of Castle Bolton at Redmire on 6th January 1987.*

No. 37172 leaves Tees Yard with the 6M41 empty limestone hopper wagons for Hardendale Quarry, Shap on 10th February 1987.

Steetley operate these 51 tonne hoppers for carrying Dolime daily from Thrislington to Hartlepool via Stillington. The wagons are cream with black lettering.

The loading bunkers dominate the railhead at Thrislington. On 11th February 1987, No. 47303 pulls the lime wagons out of the loading area.

No. 37141 arrives at Steetley's Hartlepool works on 31st October 1986 with lime and dolime.

Steetleys employ an 0-4-0 diesel-hydraulic shunter (Hunslet 7425 of 1981) at Hartlepool to move the wagons from the exchange sidings into the factory.

On 28th July 1987, No. 37096 takes the Mineralhaul 46 tonne mag. lime wagons from Ferryhill towards Thrislington.

Thompsons of Prudhoe own these side tipping PTA wagons which convey magnesium limestone to Montrose. The wagons are loaded at Ferryhill station each morning.

The mag. lime from the Ferryhill area is tripped to Tyne Yard on the 9P04 working. On 11th February 1987, No. 37138 takes two Thompsons wagons north on the ECML at Ferryhill.

On 13th May 1987, No. 08388 waits for ilmenite to be loaded into unfitted tippler wagons at Immingham Docks. Trains run when the boat docks, which on average is every two months.

One of Tioxides Ruston & Hornsby diesel-mechanical shunters stands off (probably 421418 of 1958), as a wagon is raised on the tippler.

The wagons are tipped to allow the ilmenite to pour onto underground conveyors.

Rockware Glass at Wheatley receive sand by train each day. On 23rd April 1987, No. 31116 stands on its train under the discharge shed. The traffic lights on the shed roof inform the driver when to stop or move forward.

logo on the side. The one train a day arrives with empties and departs with 33 wagons carrying 1,200 tonnes of limestone. This single line to Northallerton passes through Leyburn and Bedale before meeting the East Coast Main Line at Castle Hills Junction. At Redcar the limestone is discharged on a merry-go-round system, with 'daleks' tripping the discharge doors. The train has therefore to be hauled by locomotives fitted with slow speed control and is usually a pair of Class 20s. The empty wagons are subsequently taken back to Tees Yard for the return trip to Redmire the following morning.

British Steel at Lackenby also need limestone for steel production. This is obtained from the giant British Steel quarry at Hardendale on Shap in Cumbria. A daily train of 1,000 tonnes of limestone runs via Carlisle and Tyne Yard on the 6E43 overnight service, the empty PBA hoppers being returned on the 6M41 19.40 from Lackenby.

In the area around Ferryhill a different type of limestone is found. This is dolomite which contains both calcium carbonate and magnesium carbonate and has a wide variety of uses in steelmaking processes. At Thrislington, near Ferryhill, Steetleys have a large quarry of dolomite rock. The top strata are suitable for the steel industry and Railfreight moves the stone to various steel plants. One flow is to British Steel at Ravenscraig in Scotland in ex British Steel iron ore tipplers. Large overhead bunkers dominate the railhead at Ferryhill. The highest grade stone is sent to the on-site calcining unit and the resulting dolime (calcined dolomite) is fed into the giant bunkers to be loaded into PAA hopper wagons. There are 30 such wagons, cream in colour and with the Steetley name and logo painted in black. A further bunker holds lime which is loaded into PBA hoppers, 15 of which are on hire from CAIB.

Each weekday a Class 47 makes the trip from Thrislington to the company's sister plant at Hartlepool with 20–25 wagons of lime and dolime. The dolime is used in their special sea water magnesia process, the end products being refractory magnesia used in the lining of furnaces for steel, cement and glass making. The lime is used in the production of high grade refractory materials. Every week 3,000 to 4,000 tonnes of lime and dolime move from Thrislington to Hartlepool. There are no works shunters at Thrislington, but Hartlepool employs a Hunslet 0-4-0 diesel locomotive to pull wagons into the factory from the exchange sidings.

As well as being used for refractory magnesia and the steel industry, magnesium limestone, or mag lime, has other useful applications. Mineralhaul of Middlesbrough are transport contractors who operate a fleet of 46 tonne mineral wagons for conveying mag lime to Scotland from Tilcon's Raisby quarry and Steetley's Thrislington quarry at Ferryhill. These go to several depots including Mossend, Kittybrewster, Dundee, Craiginches and Inverurie.

The Bishop Middleham quarry near Ferryhill is operated by Thompson's of Prudhoe. They own six 60 tonne side-tipping PTA wagons which are loaded with mag lime by lorries at Ferryhill station. The company moves about 250 tonnes a week to Montrose where it is distributed to Scottish farmers by road hauliers Carnegie. All the mag lime flows from the Ferryhill area are tripped to Tyne Yard on the morning 9PO4 train to connect with Speedlink services.

One interesting sidelight is that grazing cattle, in particular Ayrshires, are susceptible to a condition known as 'grass staggers'. This is caused by a deficiency of mag-nesium and leads to the cattle shivering and staggering. To combat this, the farmers spread mag lime on the grazing pastures to give the cattle the magnesium supply they need. You might even argue that Railfreight is helping to support Scottish cattle!

One unusual working occurs at Grimsby on the south bank of the Humber. Ilmenite, a readily available black beach sand found in Australia, India and Sri Lanka, is brought into Immingham Docks in large cargo ships. It is unloaded by dockside cranes into hoppers and from there is discharged into a rake of tippler wagons (PSOs). These wagons, owned by Tioxide UK Ltd and built on former tank wagon frames, are unfitted and are only allowed to work between Immingham Docks and Tioxide's works at Pye-wipe, Grimsby. They are hauled in rakes of 35 from the docks to the factory a short distance away. Once in the plant, one of Tioxide's shunters hauls the wagons to the tippler, where, one by one, and still on a section of rail, they are secured, lifted, turned and discharged onto conveyors. Tioxide use the ilmenite to produce titanium dioxide, a high quality white paint pigment used by industry in paints, paper, plastics and textiles. The flow of ilmenite is totally dependent on the berthing of the ships at Immingham. On average, one docks every eight weeks. Locomotives have to be made available, usually at short notice, by the Immingham depot, the motive power varying between either Class 37s or Class 47s.

The glass industry in South Yorkshire uses a specially prepared sand — Chempure — for making flint glass or clear glass. This sand is delivered from British Industrial Sand at King's Lynn who wash and bleach it with acid to remove the iron. Each weekday, Rockware Glass Ltd at Wheatley, Doncaster, receives a train of 450 tonnes, and two days a week, Redfearn National Glass at Monk Bretton, Barnsley, receives 700 tonnes of sand. On those days the train is shared between the two companies until it reaches Belmont Yard at Doncaster where it is split into two sections and tripped to the appropriate company. The wagons used are two axle PAA hoppers with a 38 tonne load capacity. They are owned by BIS and have pneu-matically operated roof and bottom discharge doors. Rockware Glass also receives 450 tonnes of limestone a week from the Steetley quarry at Dowlow near Buxton. The limestone moves on Speedlink in PBA bogie hopper wagons owned and operated by Mineralhaul. From the weekly 2,250 tonnes of sand and 450 tonnes of limestone, Rockware manufactures up to 20 million glass jars!

Peakstone Ltd, who are part of the Ready Mixed Concrete (RMC) group, run a large limestone quarry at Dove Holes, near Buxton. Each weekday 800 tonnes of limestone are moved to the company's sidings at Hunslet, Leeds. The stone is unloaded from the vacuum-braked MSV open wagons by a mechanical shovel and is used both for roadstone and concrete products. The train, the 7E18 from Peak Forest, arrives at Hunslet about 14.30 hours, the empties returning to Peak Forest the same day. Peakstone also have a terminal within the Selby storage complex. Limestone is received, two, sometimes three times a week from their Dove Holes quarry. The trains of HTV hopper wagons or Peakstone's own PHA 90 tonne bogie wagons in the RMC colours, are bottom discharged onto conveyors to feed the bitumen-macadam plant. Some 1,600 tonnes of limestone are received each week.

The Chempure sand is discharged from the wagons through pneumatically operated bottom doors. The roof doors are also pneumatically operated to facilitate loading of these PAAs.

No. 45007 Taliesin draws the empty MSV limestone wagons out of the Peakstone sidings at Hunslet, Leeds on 7th August 1987.

The new Peakstone bitumen-macadam plant at Selby receives two trains of limestone from Peak Forest each week. Selby Storage's shunter (a Sentinel 0-6-0 diesel hydraulic on hire from Thomas Hill) pulls the HTV wagons through the discharge shed on 23rd June 1988.

Chapter 6
Construction

Railfreight Construction moves considerable amounts of materials in the region—bricks, concrete blocks, tiles, refuse, fly ash and aggregates. (The latter are dealt with in the Minerals chapter.) The main flow, however, is cement, Blue Circle and Castle being the major Railfreight customers in the North East.

The history of cement making in the last 20 years is one of peaks and troughs. In the late 1960s and 1970s two factors came together which led to a dramatic rise in cement production. First was the boom in pre-stressed concrete which proved cheaper than bricks and steel. Second was the sharp increase in oil prices following the Arab-Israeli War of 1973. This influenced the price of bitumen, thus making traditional bitumen-based black top macadam roads expensive to build. The road construction industry decided therefore, to use concrete instead. Although the three main UK cement manufacturers had a common price agreement, the quality of the cements did vary slightly in different parts of the country. Because of the price uniformity, the manufacturers had to find other ways of enhancing their products. Interestingly enough, cement came to be sold on colour, and in certain cases selling even hinged on the colour of the company's vans, the delivery driver's uniform and his civility! Things began to change, however. The Eastern Europeans, in particular the German Democratic Republic, entered the market. They had both a spare capacity in their home markets and a strong desire for Western currency—and their cement was cheap. Likewise, when Greece became a member of the EEC, they moved cement in bulk to large floating silos, strategically placed to seek out market opportunities in Britain. To add to the industry's problems, brick, steel and glass came back into favour for the construction of new buildings. Also, the price of oil has dropped so much of late that black top roads are again cheap to build. The result is that there is minimal growth in the home cement market and with the end of the common price agreement in 1987, companies are going through a period of retrenchment. Nevertheless, Railfreight still moves between $2^1/4$–$2^1/2$ million tonnes a year within the North East, the biggest single source being Blue Circle at Hope in the Peak District.

The works there are served by a $1^1/2$ mile privately-owned line from the British Rail exchange sidings on the Sheffield to Manchester Hope Valley line. Blue Circle produce ordinary Portland Cement from the dry kiln process, limestone and shale being the basic raw materials. Five days a week a 900 tonne train of vacuum-braked Cemflo wagons delivers to the Blue Circle Dewsbury railhead. The Cemflo is an aluminium-bodied wagon dating from the 1960s and is to be replaced at the end of 1988. Three days a week a 740 tonne train hauling 51 tonne PCA and 102 tonne PDA wagons supplies the Blue Circle railhead at Kirton Lindsey south of Scunthorpe.

Two other dedicated cement trains leave Hope daily. The first leaves with a 1,800 tonne load in up to 36 PCA wagons and drops them off at Blue Circle depots at Beeston, Syston (Leicester) and Handsworth, Birmingham. It then collects the empties in reverse order. The second train serves Widnes for the Liverpool area and Northenden for Manchester. There is also a daily Speedlink train from Peak Forest which conveys cement tripped from Hope. In addition, there are occasional specials, usually trainload, which operate if large tonnages of cement are required for a major construction project.

Hope has a fleet of 90 Cemflo PCVs for the Dewsbury Circuit, and 224 PCAs and 26 bogied PDAs for the remainder of the services. The company has two Sentinel diesel shunters which are used to move the wagons around the loading areas. They also hire a Class 08 from British Rail to pull the loaded trains the one and a half miles to the exchange sidings. Hope can produce up to 1.2 million tonnes of cement a year, Railfreight transporting between 700,000 and 800,000 tonnes.

The Blue Circle works at Eastgate in the heart of Weardale were commissioned in 1965 and have a production capacity of about 750,000 tonnes a year. Intended to serve the North of England and parts of Scotland, the works are rail-connected by an extension of the Darlington to Bishop Auckland line. The cement is stored in large silos, from which it is fed into rail or road tankers. Sentinel shunters are used to form the two daily trains. The morning train departs for Tees Yard and the afternoon train for Tyne Yard. Both are quasi-trainload operations conveying cement for Blue Circle depots at Heaton, Newcastle and Middlesbrough, and for Carlisle in the North West. The trains are split at the yards and forwarded on Speedlink to their destinations. Also included are wagons for attaching to Speedlink services conveying special cements to such destinations as Beeston, Handsworth, Bristol, Widnes, Northenden and Irving. The morning train usually has a payload of 1,300 tonnes in 35 PCA wagons and the afternoon train 1,100 tonnes. Both are hauled by Class 37s. Two hundred and sixty-five PCA wagons are allocated to the Eastgate traffic and these are maintained on site by Powell Duffryn. Some 400,000 tonnes of cement are moved by rail each year from Eastgate.

Castle Cement at Clitheroe send a trainload of cement in PCAs to either Middlesbrough or Newcastle Railway Street. The service operates as and when required but runs most weekdays in the summer months when the demand is greatest.

In the 1970s bricks were carried by rail in conventional open wagons from Peterborough and Bedford. Loaded by hand and packed in straw, the operation was very labour-intensive. New packaging methods were geared to road vehicles, with the consequence that some of the traffic was lost. British Rail did, however, have a regular forwarding of bricks on the 'Fletliner' from Stewartby to Manchester and Liverpool. This was a Freightliner service and used modern handling techniques.

Butterley Brick produce a wide range of facing bricks from their factories around the country. The bricks move on Speedlink services from a number of railheads, including a private siding at Boughton near Worksop. They are generally carried on OBAs to the so-called 'brick shops' which in the North East are located at Huddersfield and the Tyneside Central Freight depot at Gateshead. These brick shops are, in fact, Railfreight terminals which hold stocks of bricks for the company. If a customer wants to place an order for bricks, he contacts Butterley. They in turn inform Railfreight who then release the bricks to the customer. In this way Butterley is able to have a network of depots nationwide.

The PCV aluminium bodied 'Cemflo' cement wagon was ahead of its time when introduced. They have now reached the end of their working lives and are being phased out.

The 102 tonne PDA bogie cement wagons are operated by Blue Circle on a number of routes from Hope.

Blue Circle at Hope hire an 08 class diesel electric locomotive from BR to move wagons from the cement works to the exchange sidings, 1¹/₂ miles away. No. 08871 prepares a train on the 17th March 1988.

Rolls-Royce Sentinel 4-wheel diesel hydraulic shunters (10197 and 10232 of 1965) are used at Eastgate. Here the morning departure for Tees Yard is being assembled.

On 18th June 1987, No. 37185 leads the morning train from Eastgate to Tees Yard over the River Wear at Frosterley.

There are 265 PCA wagons of various designs in the Eastgate pool for the two daily trains.

At Eastgate the Blue Circle PCA wagons are repaired on site at the Powell Duffryn operated workshops.

Class 47, No. 47360 leaves the Middlesbrough Castle Cement Terminal, 28th July 1987, with the return empties to Clitheroe. This train alternates between Middlesbrough and the Castle Cement Terminal at Newcastle Railway Street.

Castle Cement (formerly Ribble Cement) use Standard Wagon built PCAs to move cement from Clitheroe to either Middlesbrough or Newcastle.

Bricks are delivered on Speedlink to the Railfreight managed 'brick shops' at Huddersfield and the Tyneside Central Freight Depot.

Redland Roof Tiles Ltd have terminals at Gateshead and Sculcoates at Hull. Roof tiles are stacked onto OBA and OAA wagons painted in the company colours of two tone green with red lettering.

At Heck, south of Selby, Plasmor produce concrete blocks for use in the building industry. A Hymac crane loads blocks into a modified OBA wagon.

Redland Rooftiles also use Speedlink to move tiles from their factory at Stirling in Scotland to their rail-connected depot at Gateshead. OBA wagons in the company's livery of two-tone green with red lettering can be seen arriving daily. The tiles are stacked on pallets for the journey and unloaded by fork lift onto road vehicles for final delivery to site. Redland also send deliveries of tiles and fixings from Rugby to their siding at Hull Sculcoates. Customers in West Yorkshire are served from the freight terminal at Dewsbury.

One of Railfreight Construction's success stories is the movement of concrete blocks from Plasmor's private sidings just off the East Coast Main Line at Heck, north of Doncaster. The two sidings were opened in March 1987. Plasmor manufacture the concrete blocks from furnace bottom ash and small quantities of fly ash obtained from the nearby power stations of Eggborough and Drax. They are used for both housing and commercial buildings. Speedlink enabled Plasmor to break into the London and South East market where the major building developments are taking place. The blocks are delivered to depots at Bow, Biggleswade and Willesden, final distribution being by road. Further depots are planned and one at Widnes in the North West is already being built.

The blocks produced at Heck are carried by road to the nearby rail sidings where a Hymac crane lifts them onto OBA wagons. The sidings can accommodate 44 OBAs which have been modified by extending the height of the end boards to allow the blocks to be double-stacked. Some of the wagons on hire from Railfreight have been painted in the Plasmor colours of green and orange with a white centre

stripe. A Class 31 usually collects the wagons from Heck in the late afternoon and trips them to Belmont Yard, Doncaster, where they are placed on the relevant Speedlink trains. About 3,000 tonnes of blocks are moved by Railfreight each week from Heck and the possibility of future trainload working cannot be ruled out.

Another success story for Railfreight Construction in recent years is the disposal of household refuse. Rubbish has to be got rid of and, with time, the traditional local quarry sites are being filled. This means that councils are having to look further afield to find disposal sites. Land reclamation schemes are one area where councils can dispose of their rubbish and help reclaim land scarred by previous industrial workings. As sites become scarce, Railfreight will no doubt have in mind that it may not be the right decision to lift tracks from a disused quarry since it may have a second life as a landfill site — always subject to planning permission being granted, of course.

In late 1987 Cobra Railfreight of Wakefield began receiving rubbish from Greater Manchester. Wimpey Waste Management Ltd suffered a delay to a planning application to extend the use of their quarry near Manchester as a refuse disposal point. As they were under contract to dispose of the waste from Manchester, they could not let the rubbish pile up whilst they awaited the outcome. They had to find an interim site and one was chosen at Woodkirk near Dewsbury. The rubbish is transported from Manchester on PFA bogie flat wagons, with three orange and white 20 foot containers to each wagon. Each container holds ap-

On 20th January 1988, No. 31311 waits in Plasmor's sidings to gain the East Coast Main Line to Belmont Yard. From there the wagons find their way to depots at Bow, Biggleswade and Willesden.

One unusual working that commenced in late 1987, was the two daily trains of refuse from Manchester to the Cobra depot at Wakefield. On 6th November 1987, No. 47344 uncouples from the morning train that has arrived from Northenden.

A container handling vehicle unloads the containerised rubbish from the train at Cobra's Wakefield depot.

No. 47211 enters the power station loop at West Burton on 29th November 1986, with 48 CSA Presflo wagons for loading with pulverised fly ash.

proaching 16 tonnes of waste and each wagon has a gross weight of 60 tonnes. Both wagons and containers are owned by the Greater Manchester Waste Disposal Authority. Two trains a day deliver waste to Wakefield, the morning train conveying 14 wagons and originating at the GMWDA refuse disposal point at Northenden, the afternoon train starting at Bredbury with 14 wagons also. Cobra's own handling vehicles remove the containers from the train and place them onto a fleet of waiting road vehicles operated by Wimpey. They are then moved the short distance to the site for tipping. Some 1,200 tonnes of waste is handled by Cobra every day. The trains rejoice in the name of 'Bin-Liners'!

A well-known landfill site is the old London Brick Works at Fletton near Peterborough. Here, pulverised fly ash (PFA) is used to restore land to agricultural use. PFA is produced at power stations from the combustion of pulverised coal and is separated from boiler flue gases by mechanical collectors and electrostatic precipitators.

West Burton Power Station's burn of five million tonnes of coal a year produces some 750,000 tonnes of fly ash. From Monday to Saturday two or three trains a day collect the fly ash in Presflo wagons and deliver it to Fletton. The train has a total weight of about 1,700 tonnes and is made up of 48 wagons each holding 19 tonnes. Although the movement from West Burton will continue for some time, the building of a second power station there will mean that the PFA will be used in its construction and deliveries to Fletton will therefore cease.

The latest landfill site in the North East is at Glews Hollow, Goole. Railfreight is to move 600,000 tonnes of colliery spoil from Hatfield near Doncaster in four trainloads a day. The wagons will be sidetipping with a 68 tonne payload and built by Standard Wagon.

Once loaded the train heads for the CEGB landfill site at Fletton, Peterborough.

Chapter 7
Chemicals

The basic raw materials used in the chemical industries are salt, petroleum and natural gas. The industries generally grew up near the raw materials, coastal sites often being chosen either for facilitating the import of crude oil or for the export of products.

The main chemical complexes within the North East are at Billingham, Wilton, Hull and Immingham. The ICI plant at Billingham, which is one of the world's largest, is chiefly concerned with the production of fertilisers. ICI at Wilton manufacture the raw materials for man-made fibres, chemicals and plastics, BP Chemicals at Hull produce industrial alcohols and Norsk Hydro at Immingham produce fertilisers. All are served by Railfreight.

At one time the amount of chemicals traffic was predictable, companies regularly using rail to move trainloads between complexes on a regular basis as part of their industrial processes. Trainload traffic has, however, decreased over the years. Today more than 50% of chemicals traffic in the North East moves on Speedlink. Trainload traffic tends to be small and is now mainly confined to the movement of hazardous chemicals. The latter only move in trainload when they are incompatible with other traffics. It is possible to mix chemicals traffic on Speedlink workings within the train formation, ensuring, for instance, that corrosive traffic is not put next to explosives. The TOPS computer would not allow this to happen since each commodity has a code. If two wagons are found to be incompatible, alarm bells ring. Depending on the loads carried, this may be solved by putting a pre-determined number of compatible wagons between the two, thus allowing them to travel on the same train. Sometimes, however, this is not possible and it is often easier to move the chemicals as a special small trainload.

The growth area for Railfreight is the carriage of plastics and their associated raw materials, and in the movement of pharmaceuticals. These are high-value loads, some being worth as much as £1,000 per tonne. Since the transportation of chemicals can be a sensitive issue, it might be assumed that a high percentage goes by rail. This is not so, for Railfreight's share of chemicals traffic nationwide is only about 10%. Moreover, there is constant competition from road, coastal shipping and pipelines. The loss of some liquids and gases traffic has led to customers taking out their rail sidings. Today it would be far too expensive for the same customer to revert to rail for the costs of a railhead to handle hazardous substances can far outweigh the benefits of moving it by rail.

At one time ten year contracts for the movement of chemicals were common, but are now unheard of. Such is the need to keep costs to a minimum that Section 8 grants are rarely secured for these traffics. To ensure a stable future, Railfreight will have to keep the chemicals traffic it already has, and with the aid of the private sector wagon hirers will have to be able to move quickly to win short-term movements. The Channel Tunnel will no doubt help here, as some of the chemicals companies see Europe as their market place. Companies in the market for a particular chemical shop around and look for the cheapest buy. This, however, has it drawbacks, since a fluctuating exchange rate can make trading difficult. For instance, a product like methanol, which is produced by ICI at Billingham, is also produced on the Continent. A company wanting methanol in this country may buy 'on spot' in Rotterdam, ship it to this country and move it from the port by rail. The following week, the methanol price in Rotterdam may rise, therefore the Continental companies might want to buy from ICI in this country. This is one of the reasons why methanol wagons can be seen all over the network. It is in this type of 'spot' buying that Railfreight is establishing itself, adapting quickly to the needs of both the company and the market.

Formerly most chemicals tank wagons had mild steel barrels and throughout the life of the wagon were used for one chemical only. Today, however, many tank wagons are manufactured with stainless steel barrels. The advantage is that the empty tanks can be purged and a different chemical carried. Mild steel barrels are not so versatile. Tank cleaning facilities are available at most large chemical complexes, but if necessary British Rail can undertake the work at Thornaby. The initial cost of a stainless steel chemicals tank wagon can be high, but it has a longer life than the equivalent road tanker. The life of the latter is reckoned to be between five and seven years, whilst the rail tanker's is fifteen. And with road you still have to buy the motive power!

We have earlier indicated the hazardous nature of certain chemicals and it is argued by some that rail is the safest form of transport for these substances over land. This is because British Rail insist on absolute control over the movements. Certainly, some of the chemicals transported by rail are very dangerous, whilst others are totally inert and need no special handling. For chemical companies the most critical times are on loading and discharge. Some highly dangerous chemicals are loaded in a completely sealed-off area and before the wagons can proceed, they have to be washed down and the loading area made safe. For the movement of hazardous chemicals, British Rail require a 'certificate of closure'. This is a signed document stating that the wagon being released to British Rail is sealed and safe to travel.

Some pressurised tankers are designed to vent off if the pressure builds up. This acts as a sort of safety valve. Wagons carrying chemicals of this nature are generally classed as hazardous, but the leakage itself is not a significant hazard. Railway workers are aware of these wagons which carry such chemicals as carbon dioxide and nitrogen.

All hazardous chemicals wagons have labels, usually orange, with a series of letters and numbers. These inform the emergency services what the chemical is and how they should tackle any spillages. The United Nations number, the four figure number in the centre panel, will identify the chemical.

Some hazardous chemicals moving around the North East in trainload have speed restrictions imposed on them. This can be as little as 35 mph in some cases and could disrupt passenger services on the East Coast Main Line. These trains, however, tend to run at quiet times between yards and have barrier vehicles both front and rear. For some loads British Rail insist on closed vans forming the barrier vehicles, whilst for others, specially-built steel barrier vehicles are used. These are intended to minimise the effects of a collision or a fire on the locomotive, thereby preventing the chemicals wagons being penetrated whilst in transit. A guard usually travels in a guard's van at the rear of the train.

On 10th February 1987, No. 47285 brings the 6O49 Haverton Hill to Eastleigh Speedlink train into Tees Yard. The wagons conveyed are a bogie sulphuric acid tank, three caustic soda tanks and the remainder methanol tanks. The train splits once in the yard and the wagons are placed on their respective Speedlink services.

Methanol tank wagons have a dove grey tank barrel with red solebar. This TTB wagon No. 54858 can carry 32.7 tonnes of product.

Liquid nitrogen is used in the frozen food industry and has other applications. TEA cryogenic tank wagons operated by BOC are red and white and are frequently seen in the North East.

No. 31417 waits to depart from Seal Sands with three acetic acid tank wagons.

Liquid carbon dioxide is carried under pressure in TTA wagons to various locations on Speedlink. Some, like this example, No. 53207 have the Distillers name on the side.

For some dangerous chemicals barrier vehicles have to be used to prevent damage to tank wagons. This PXA wagon No. 4917 is a purpose-built barrier vehicle. It is of all-metal construction and is painted grey.

The newer type of Transfesa wagons are used for carrying pure terephthalic acid (P.T.A.) from ICI Wilton via the train ferries to Spain and Portugal.

Soda ash is delivered to Rockware Glass at Knottingley and Wheatley in PCA wagons from Northwich.

Seals Sands Storage is a rail-connected chemical and petroleum product tank farm. No. 31417 reverses two Hays 100 tonne sulphuric acid wagons into the depot.

A German registered tank wagon owned by VTG. This example was carrying glycol. Continental tank wagons are a common sight in the North East. Note the hooks on the solebar above the wheels used for securing the vehicle on the ferry.

This German Federal Railways tank wagon with sun canopy conveys amines (various compounds derived from ammonia) in a gas form from ICI Billingham to the Continent.

Owned by Simotra (now CAIB) these tank wagons carry hexamethylenediamene into Wilton daily from France. The tanks have heating elements in them to prevent the substance solidifying.

On 22nd June 1987, No. 37128 heads the BP Saltend to Doncaster Belmont Yard 'vinegar tanks' through Kirk Sandall.

This Algeco 45 tonne tank wagon, No. 49368, stands at Seal Sands. The United Nations number on the Hazchem warning panel will lead to the identification of the substance. In this case No. 2789 refers to acetic acid — hence 'vinegar tanks'.

Hydrocyanic acid (HCN) is collected from BASF at Seal Sands and taken to ICI at Billingham. No. 31311 heads for BASF with the empties on 20th May 1988.

No. 37113 passes through Tyne Yard with the 8X98 HCN empties to Grangemouth on 23rd August 1988. Barrier vehicles are used front and rear, a guard has to be carried and the train has a speed restriction imposed on it.

A CAIB owned anhydrous ammonia tank wagon operated by ICI, stands outside an ammonia plant at Billingham. The wagons are white with an orange band, indicating that the substance carried is under pressure.

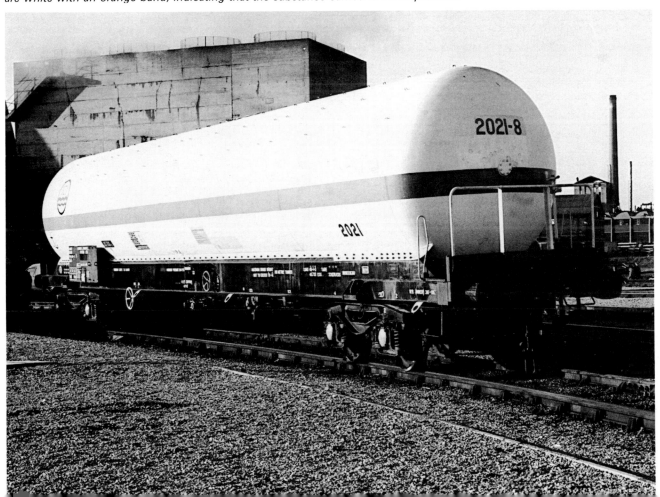

The line from Stockton to Ferryhill is used for freight only and occasional diversions. No. 47363 Billingham Enterprise *passes Carlton Grange with empty ammonia wagons on 28th June 1988. Destinations for these wagons are Severnside, Leith and Grangemouth.*

Should an incident occur, the driver can warn from the front and the guard from the rear. Neither needs to pass the suspect wagon.

Already a large amount of chemicals traffic from the North East moves to and from the Continent on the train ferries. Most chemical complexes in Europe are rail-connected and, with the opening of the Channel Tunnel, trainloads of inert chemicals will be able to reach mainland Europe much more easily. The more dangerous chemicals may not be allowed through the Tunnel and these will probably continue to use the open decks of the train ferries.

The chemicals flows are too numerous to mention here. The following tables will serve as a guide to what can be seen, but because of the possibilities of industrial espionage, not all the chemicals have been listed.

Fertiliser

In the late 1970s British Rail lost some chemicals and fertiliser customers when companies switched to palletised distribution. The old BR van fleet could not accommodate

the loading of pallets by fork lifts since the latter could not load around corners of vans which had only a small door in the middle. The result was that companies changed to road distribution. It was only with the new air-braked fleet and the expansion of the private sector wagon leasing and hiring companies in recent years that companies have cautiously begun to return to rail. Those which have, have found that Railfreight is much changed. The wagon payloads are much greater, loading is now extremely simple, and with TOPS, the control of wagons is far more efficient. Fertiliser traffic is one area where companies are returning to rail and investing heavily in terminal facilities.

The main producers in the North East are ICI at Billingham, Brit-Ag at Barton-on-Humber which is owned by ICI, and Norsk Hydro at Immingham. Norsk, whose complete fertiliser production takes place on the one site, is well situated at Immingham Docks to receive its raw materials by ship.

At Billingham ICI produce raw materials in the form of ammonia and phosphorus. They also produce ammonia for other fertiliser companies. Trainloads of ammonia can be seen travelling from Billingham to ICI's sister plant at Severnside, to BP at Grangemouth and to SAI fertilisers at Leith in Scotland. The wagons used are VTG and CAIB-owned and are leased to ICI. They have a gross weight of about 80 tonnes and can carry 50 tonnes of ammonia. The wagons are bogied and are either white or grey with a horizontal orange band around the middle. This denotes that the substance carried is under pressure. These trains usually travel with a barrier vehicle both front and rear.

The potash used by ICI is moved from Boulby and delivered to Cobra Railfreight's Middlesbrough terminal where it is put into road vehicles for final delivery to Billingham. Some finished fertiliser in 50kg bags, ½ tonne and 1 tonne 'big bags' moves out of Middlesbrough Goods on pre-shrink pallets to various destinations. The greater part of ICI's finished product is, however, despatched by road.

Norsk Hydro produce various grades of fertiliser on the site of the old Fison's works which Norsk took over in 1982. In a highly competitive market, Norsk invested money both in the plant and in a rail distribution system. It was considered that rail was best suited to a single source production and an intensive final delivery system. The fertiliser is packed in 'big bags' or on pre-shrink pallets and is loaded directly into the wagons by fork lifts in their covered warehouses. Two works shunters move the wagons in and out of the loading area.

In conjunction with Railfreight and ISIS Link Ltd, who organise Norsk Hydro's distribution system, a number of rail-served 'superstores' were established throughout the country. New handling and distribution warehouses were set up at Immingham. ISIS began using VTG 54 tonne wagons and French-built curtain-sided bogie wagons with the Norsk Hydro name and logo on the side. The VTG wagons have now gone and have been replaced by 62 tonne Cargowaggons. These have aluminium sides and roof with the Norsk and ISIS names on them. A morning and an afternoon train is despatched from Norsk to the 'superstores' at Leith and Severnside respectively. A midday train takes wagons to Belmont Yard for the Speedlink services. On average about 30 bogie wagons leave Norsk by rail each day, Railfreight moving around 350,000 tonnes each year.

UKF Fertilisers of Ince in Cheshire have a rail-connected storage and distribution depot at Hopetown, Darlington. They receive one booked train each week. The fertiliser moves in UKF-designed 72 tonne gross bogie vans with their name on the side. VTG 54 tonne wagons and Procor 45 tonne curtain-sided wagons are also used. The train is split into two sections at Darlington so that it can be accommodated in the limited length siding at Hopetown. The wagons are then tripped in batches to the depot for unloading before being returned to Ince.

One of the own-brand fertiliser distributors, Humber Fertilisers, moves occasional loads to the South of England from the Hull Dairycoates rail terminal. Other rail-served terminals dealing with fertiliser distribution are Smallers at Immingham, Stockton Haulage and Cobra Railfreight at Middlesbrough and Wakefield. Selby Storage and Freight Company, in addition to handling common-named fertilisers, also handles calcined seaweed from the South West.

Phosphoric acid is used in the production of fertiliser. Occasional trains can be seen in the North East area. This turquoise coloured 51 tonne wagon stained white with chemical was photographed at Immingham Docks.

Pallets of fertiliser are loaded onto a VTG ferrywagon at Norsk Hydro works at Immingham. VTGs have been superseded by larger capacity Cargowaggons.

This French built 58 tonne fertiliser wagon has curtain sides which fold back fully, when primed by the hydraulic system located at the ends. Colours of the curtains are blue or black with yellow or white lettering.

Urea is moved in prilled form (pellets) from ICI Billingham to various locations in 51 tonne PAA wagons painted black with white lettering and red solebar.

Chemical Traffic in the North East

Company	Chemical	Use	F – From T – To	Wagon type	Colour scheme	How moved	Trainload T/L Speedlink S/L
Egger UK	Amino resin	Glue for chipboard	F Ciba-Geigy Duxford	TTB 45 tonne tank wagon 2 axle	Light blue Ciba-Geigy name on side	Liquid	S/L
Steetley Hartlepool	Chemical magnesias	Rubber, plastics and others	T Portugal	Transfesa	Blue/steel with Transfesa name	Bagged Chemicals	S/L
Seal Sands Storage	Various – incl. caustic soda and sulphuric acid	Storage for customers	T & F various	Various tank wagons – some 100 tonne bogie	Various	Various	T/L & S/L
BP Chemicals Hull (Saltend)	Acetic anhydride various industrial alcohols	Various chemical processes	T Spondon, Teesside Baglan Bay	45 tonne 2 axle lagged	Stainless steel; STS or Algeco name on side	Liquids	S/L
Rockware Glass Wheatley and Doncaster	Soda ash	Glass	F Northwich	PCA 2 axle pressure discharge	Wedgewood blue with Rockware name & logo on side	Powder	S/L
ICI Billingham	Urea	Resins	T Various	PAA 2 axle hopper	Black with ICI logo on side red solebar	Prills (Pellets)	S/L
	Methanol	Resins and petrol additive	T Various	TTA 2 axle tanks	Dove grey; ICI logo; red solebar	Liquid	T/L & S/L
	Carbon Dioxide	Fizzy drinks Brewing industry	T Various some for Distillers	TTA 2 axle pressurised tanks	White, horizontal stripe; some Distillers name on side	Gas	S/L
	Hydrocyanic acid	Synthetic fibres and fumigant	F BASF Seal Sands F BP Grangemouth	TUA 2 axle pressurised tanks	White – orange stripe – ICI logo	Gas	T/L with barrier vehicle
	Amines (Various forms)	synthetic fibres	T France Switzerland E. & W.Germany	2 axle & 4 axle continental tanks – various types	White/grey with orange stripe	Gas or Liquid	S/L
	Ammonia	Fertiliser production	T Various	80t gross bogie tanks	White or grey with orange stripe	Gas	T/L
ICI Callerton	Explosives (various)	Explosives	F Various	various Railfreight owned	Railfreight colours	–	T/L

85

Company	Chemical	Use	F – From T – To	Wagon type	Colour scheme	How moved	Trainload T/L Speedlink S/L
ICI Wilton	Adepic acid	Manufacture of Nylon fibre	T Bridg-water	VDA vans	Railfreight colours	Bagged	S/L
	Pure teraphthalic acid (PTA)	Ingredient of Terylene	T Spain T Portugal T Jugoslavia	Transfesa and Cargowaggon	Various	Powder	S/L
	Hexamethylene-diamene	Manufacture of Nylon	F France	Continental bogie tanks with heating elements	Grey/steel some have Rhône-Poulenc on side	Liquid	S/L
Immingham Storage	Various includes caustic soda	Storage for customers	T & F Various	Various tank wagons	Various	Liquids & Gas	S/L & T/L
Ciba-Geigy Grimsby	Chemical Intermediates	Various	T Switzer-land	Continental tanks and Cargowaggon	Various	Liquids & Powders	S/L
Courtaulds Grimsby	Caustic soda	For viscose Rayon plant	F ICI Runcorn	TTA 45 tonne 2 axle	Black with orange sole-bar; ICI name on side	Liquid	T/L
Tioxide UK Grimsby	Titanium dioxide	Paints and Plastics	T Jugoslavia	Cargowaggons bogie (IPB)	Steel; Cargo-waggon name on side	Powder	S/L

No. 47362 arrives at ICI Billingham on the 11th January 1988 with a train of empty ammonia wagons. Destinations for these wagons are Severnside, Leith and Grangemouth.

Chapter 8
Freightliners Ltd

Although containers have been used on rail for several decades, it was not until the 1960s that the first container trains ran between London and Glasgow. Intended to help rationalize the wagonload business, the concept was that non-bulk goods were to move in larger units over greater distances and with fewer or no intermediate stops. The thinking at that time was that the newly-created Freightliner should become British Rail's intermodal arm. The future looked rosy, but the best laid plans . . . !

The economic estimates of the mid-1960s happily assumed a 4% growth rate — which was never attained — and in addition failed to foresee the growth in the motorway network and the rising strength of road competition. In 1964 the maximum weight for lorries rose from 24 to 32 tons, thereby making it increasingly difficult for rail to pick up the more lucrative non-bulk traffics. Although Britain was the pioneer in containerised rail transport, the intention initially was to serve the domestic market. The major stimulus for using containers in continental Europe, however, came in response to the changes in maritime trade. Freightliner, likewise, adapted to market forces. The outcome is that today, 85-90% of Freightliner traffic is intended for transit over water — to Northern Ireland, Europe or further afield — the domestic market share now being quite small.

It has been said that Freightliner is an extension of the mgr concept in that it has to have specialised handling equipment, specialised wagons, and trains running between fixed points. The latter are made up of 5-wagon sets which are themselves permanently coupled. Every wagon is expected to make at least one revenue-earning journey a day, and although fixed formations are generally kept, they are not adhered to as rigidly as in mgr operations. The wagons are 60ft in length and can take 2 x 30ft, 3 x 20ft or a 40ft and a 20ft container. They have small diameter wheels enabling them to carry the 8ft 6in high containers. The maximum carrying weight of a wagon is 62 tonnes and the maximum train length is 30 wagons, that is, six rakes of five wagons, although fewer are carried over steeply graded routes such as Shap. The containers, or boxes as they are known, come in different lengths (20ft, 30ft and 40ft) and have a capacity of up to 2,400 cubic feet. Some are open top, though most are enclosed. Some are curtain-sided, others allow access on three sides. Some are adapted to take a large plastic bag for bulk liquids or powders, whilst others are purpose-built metal tanks.

Although owned by the British Railways Board, Freightliners Ltd is not a sector of British Rail and the accounts are separate. From April 1987, however, Freightliner has been charged for haulage as a rail sector on the basis of cost attribution. They have what might be termed an arm's length relationship with British Rail.

A criticism levelled in the past at Freightliner is that they duplicate what Railfreight does and therefore compete with Speedlink. Though there is an element of competition, it is very marginal. The activities are clearly delineated and

Freightliner containers are to be seen in many shapes and sizes. These tank containers convey chemicals.

The FGA container flat wagons can carry two 30 foot containers or a combination of 20, 30 and 40 foot boxes.

On 22nd June 1987, No. 47157 arrives at Leeds Freightliner Terminal with the 4E76 train from Southampton.

differentiated and broad agreements exist between Freightliner and British Rail. One, for instance, is that Railfreight will carry coal; which is why you can see Russell's containers going to and from British Coal. Another is that anything which goes deep sea in a box is Freightliner's. These agreements are to ensure that there is no competition which would be to the detriment of the corporate body. Basically, Freightliners buy haulage from British Rail. They also have maintenance done by the DM & EE, heavy maintenance being carried out by BRML.

Freightliner had a relationship with another BR subsidiary, Sealink, until it was privatised. The latter operated ferries used by Freightliner from Holyhead to Dublin and Belfast, and to the Continent from Harwich to Zeebrugge. After privatisation a mutually satisfactory contract could not be agreed on the Harwich — Zeebrugge route and operations were switched to the Felixstowe — Zeebrugge route using a different shipping company, Comar Ltd. The Irish service is still being used, though of course, the revenues no longer go to British Rail. Formerly about 50% of Freightliner's expenditure went to British Rail, but now it is barely 40%.

Prior to 16th April 1987 Freightliner had four terminals in the North East area: Newcastle, Stockton, Leeds and Hull. As part of its restructuring the company closed Newcastle and Hull, leaving only Leeds and Stockton. The Leeds depot has been operational since 1967 and is situated on eleven acres of land at Stourton. Handling 300-350 containers a day for six days a week, Leeds is a medium-sized terminal

Leeds is a medium size terminal, handling some 300 – 350 containers a day, for six days a week.

The Leeds terminal is sited next to an Inland Clearance Depot, with customs facilities and run by Containerbase. These odd-looking vehicles ferry containers between the clearance depot and the terminal.

On 27th August 1988, No. 47105 pulls away from the Leeds Freightliner Terminal with the Saturday morning Leeds-Rugby-Tilbury service.

Nos 37178 and 37104 about to leave Stockton with a lightly loaded train for Felixstowe on 28th June 1988.

which has fortunately taken over much of the Hull traffic. The principal domestic customer is the Post Office.

Ninety per cent of the Leeds traffic is deep sea. Seven trains a day leave there for Stratford, Tilbury, Stockton, Southampton MCT and Felixstowe, the number of wagons hauled varying between 15 and 20. It is planned to designate certain depots as customs clearance points, Willesden, for example, being chosen for the London area. Leeds has the advantage being sited next to an Inland Clearance Depot owned by Containerbase. Since an ICD has a customs clearance facility, this will be of considerable advantage when the Channel Tunnel opens. At the moment Freightliner is already running a train a day in direct from Southampton and no doubt this will increase after 1993.

Occupying 19 1/2 acres of land, Stockton became operational in 1967. Since the closure of Newcastle, Stockton now takes all the Freightliner traffic from the area. The depot handles over 28,000 containers a year, the principal flows coming from ICI, the Post Office, British Steel and the Scottish & Newcastle Breweries. About 70% of the traffic emanates from ICI and with Wilton investing heavily in its overseas markets — no doubt with an eye partly on the Channel Tunnel — a decision has been taken to transfer the Stockton operation to a 15 acre site at ICI Wilton. The projected cost of the move will be £2 1/4 million but Freightliner is hoping to secure a 50% grant from the European Regional Development Fund. ICI will benefit as they will be able to use the 30 tonne gross laden weight containers which are at present not allowed on British roads. These will now be loaded directly onto wagons on site. Freightliner will gain from the additional traffics which will go to the Far Eastern and European markets. Moreover, Freightliner's other customers in the area will gain from the better facilities and the extra trains run. The new terminal will be known as Cleveland Depot and is expected to be open by the end of 1988.

Both Cleveland and the favourably-sited Stourton will offer local companies excellent opportunities for transporting their products swiftly and efficiently to the Continent when the Tunnel opens in 1993. It is reckoned that 70-75% of business will come from areas north and west of London. Willesden, and possibly Crewe, will be the hubs of the Channel Tunnel Freightliner operations, and estimated transit times are 12 hours London–Paris, 24 hours Liverpool–Cologne and 36 hours Leeds–Milan. Even today Freightliner can compete with road on the shorter hauls but it is on the medium and long distance journeys that the company comes into its own. Certainly Freightliner will be brought firmly into the long-haul market. Even from London the nearest industrial area on the Continent is 175 miles away in Northern France, and the distances from Yorkshire and Teesside to Lille or Paris or the Ruhr are well beyond the minimum necessary to compete with road. It is perhaps ironic that road haulage will now have the mode switch for they will be the ones getting on and off trains at the Tunnel's entrance and exit. Freightliner will run straight through!

At present Freightliner cannot run into Dover or Folkestone because of clearance limitations in Kent. To be able to carry the 8ft 6in high by 2.5m wide containers to the Tunnel mouth at Folkestone will require work costing approximately £11 million. In addition, the company is intending to renew about half of its 1,600 wagons. Built between 1966 and 1976 they are proving costly to repair. Three types of wagon are being considered. The first is a straight replacement of the existing wagon and these platforms will be the main carriers of the containers. The second type being evaluated is the low track force bogie wagon which will carry up to 82 tonnes. Thirdly, there is the small-wheeled low platform wagon which will enable Freightliner to carry 9ft 6in high containers and still remain within the British Rail loading gauge. All will have a maximum speed of 75mph. Neither should it be forgotten that Freightliner is the third-largest road haulier in the country. The projected three-fold increase in unit loads in the first year of the Channel Tunnel's opening will give the company the opportunity to offer a high quality door-to-door service.

Freightliners Ltd has now merged with Speedlink to form Railfreight Distribution.

Freightliner can be a door-to-door package, using their own vehicles to deliver containers from the rail terminals. Freightliner is the third largest road haulier in the country.

Chapter 9
Wagons and TOPS

In the North East there are two wagon builders, RFS Engineering Ltd at Doncaster, and Procor Engineering Ltd at Horbury, Wakefield. Doncaster has long been associated with wagon building and repairs and Doncaster Wagon Works was previously the wagon builder and repair section of British Rail's Doncaster Works. In October 1987 a management buy-out of the wagon building and repair shops saw the birth of RFS Engineering Ltd. The new company is continuing to design, manufacture and overhaul railway wagons and other rolling stock both for Railfreight and the private sector.

Specialising in wheel overhauls and the fitting of new tyres, RFS have, since their inception, completed the carry-over order of 124 new CDA hopper wagons built for Railfreight for use by English China Clays Ltd in Cornwall. They have also won substantial contracts for the refurbishment of wagons for the private sector and for Railfreight.

At Horbury Junction, Wakefield, Procor Engineering Ltd, which is part of the American Marmon group, has its base. Procor took over the former Charles Roberts works where they design and build specialist freight wagons, including pressurised chemical vessels. These are built to exacting standards with all-welded seams which are x-ray tested. One of Procor's most interesting developments is the small-wheeled bogie freight wagon. The advantages of this vehicle are in effectively increasing the British Rail loading gauge to permit the piggy-backing of trailers and some road vehicles and for Freightliner to be able to carry the larger, 9ft6in high deep sea containers.

A fine example of a Procor-built vehicle is the revolutionary 102 tonne aluminium-bogie aggregate wagon for Foster Yeoman. Further well-known vehicles are the much-used 51 tonne two-axle hoppers operated by ARC, Tilcon and Tarmac; caustic soda wagons for ICI, two axle pressure discharge cement wagons for Blue Circle and Rugby Cement, 100 tonne petrol tankers for Total and the Procar 80 car transporter. These wagon types can often be seen at Healey Mills Yard, either stored, waiting to go into works for repair or maintenance, or as brand-new wagons ready for despatch.

Railfreight's policy of not building new wagons — the English China Clay wagons are an exception — has allowed private wagon owners to come to the forefront, particularly in the hiring and leasing business. Companies such as Tiger, Railease, Tiphook, VTG (UK) Ltd and CAIB have large fleets of wagons, CAIB alone having some 3,300 in their UK fleet. Wagons from Continental hirers such as Cargowaggon and Transfesa are often seen in the North East and vehicles belonging to European railways also move around the system.

Before 1975 British Rail had problems in keeping track of its large and varied wagon fleets. Knowing exactly where each wagon was at any given time was virtually impossible. In 1975 British Rail introduced its TOPS (Total Operations Processing System) computer. It was based on the system used by the Southern Pacific Railroad in the USA which British Rail bought and adapted to suit its own needs. The American system was very basic but the TOPS computer of today has developed into an advanced and sophisticated piece of equipment. Amongst other things it can monitor wagons, passenger coaches, departmental stock and locomotives as well as plan their maintenance. Ringing a

company to find out how many wagons they have on site is a thing of the past. Gone, too, is the practice of the area freight assistant looking out onto the yard and guessing how many wagons are there. No longer can a company keep wagons for storage purposes without TOPS knowing about it. Overnight, TOPS revolutionised the whole of the British Rail network.

Exact numbers and types of wagons in each siding and yard can now be monitored with accuracy. This led to a massive reduction in the British Rail-owned fleet, since with planned maintenance of each wagon, more use could be made of each wagon. Consequently the wagon availability figures rose. To understand in a more practical way how TOPS operates, let us follow the progress of one wagon on its Speedlink journey.

Western Softwoods, a large timber processor, have bought timber from the Forestry Commission in North Yorkshire and they want to move it to their sawmills at Newbridge-on-Wye in mid-Wales. The company has chosen to use rail for the long haul and road vehicles for the short hauls to and from the railheads. First they request the Bristol Railfreight office for an empty wagon to be placed at Middlesbrough Goods Railfreight Terminal, having previously stated the commodity and the quantity of timber to be moved. The order is fed into TOPS by the Bristol TOPS office and the computer allocates a wagon to the customer. As the order is not large enough for trainload, it will travel by Speedlink. The local area freight office, in this case Middlesbrough, is informed of the order and that a wagon has been despatched for that traffic. It has been decided that an OBA wagon will be used for the timber. In the meantime, Western Softwoods contact one of their north eastern road hauliers to move the cut timber from Dalby Forest to the nearest Railfreight depot, Middlesbrough Goods. Western Softwoods are not rail-connected so the final delivery will be by road from the Railfreight depot at Hereford.

The empty wagon is placed for the customer

The empty wagon is now placed in the Railfreight terminal at Middlesbrough and the chargeman there informs the TOPS office at Middlesbrough that the empty wagon is in position. TOPS is updated so that the wagon's state and location is available should an enquiry regarding the wagon need to be started. The wagon we shall follow is a Railfreight-owned OBA. This is a 31 tonne gross open wagon with drop sides used for the conveyance of general merchandise.

Our wagon is allocated TOPS number 110798 and this number can be found on the TOPS information panel on the side of the wagon. (See accompanying figure.) The information on an international wagon is different in appearance, but the information conveyed is similar.

From the three letters OBA, O indicates that it is an open wagon and B that it is an open wagon with turnover bolster, with a gross weight of between 30.5 and 31.5 tonnes. The third letter, A, refers to the brake type, in this case air-braked only.

Our wagon is 31 tonnes gross: the tare weight is 14,650kg and the user can carry 16,350kg of merchandise in the wagon.

A management buy-out of the BREL Doncaster Wagon Works led to the formation of RFS Engineering Ltd. The company are continuing in the production and overhaul of wagons.

No. 08607 hauls BDA wagons for repair into the RFS complex.

RFS specialise in wheel overhauls and the fitting of new tyres.

All types of repair and overhauls are carried out in the RFS workshops.

When RFS emerged, it had to complete the BREL contract for 124 CDA china clay hoppers. Wagon No. 375093 stands outside the works prior to delivery.

At Procor's Horbury Works, welding takes place on an Amey Roadstone 51 tonne PGA hopper wagon.

The future lies with the small-wheeled bogie to increase the effectiveness of the BR loading gauge. This vehicle has been developed by Procor. A great deal of interest has been shown, not only in this country but by overseas also.

This PVB van was built by Procor. It is in the livery of 'Ben Chairs' of Somerset and can carry 35.85 tonnes.

One of the recent growth areas in wagon building is in the construction of two axle container carrying vehicles. This PFA was built by Procor UK Ltd for containerised coal traffic.

An example of an Italian State Railway (83 FS) Inter Frigo refrigerated wagon at Viking Shipping, Selby.

This Belgian rolled top wagon at Sheffield Freight Centre was conveying refractory bricks to Belgium .

Transfesa operate a number of different wagons into this country. This is a curtain-sided bogie wagon at Tyneside Central Freight Depot with traffic from British Alcan for the Continent.

Tiphook have invested heavily in rail wagons. This is one of their 90 tonne gross, curtain-sided wagons. British Steel use a number of these within the North East.

Grain wagons can be seen at Gainsborough, Berwick and occasionally at Newcastle TCFD. Traffic also passes through the area from East Anglia to Scotland, often in these 58 tonne Grainflow polybulks.

The wagon information panel indicates the type of wagon – OBA, its carrying capacity and tare weight and the individual wagon number, 110798.

A wagon label showing the type of load and destination is placed on the wagon solebar.

On 21st January 1988 Thornaby shunter No. 08774 places OBA wagons 110716 and 110798 in 'up' siding number 14 at Tees Yard. The chargeman at the yard notifies the TOPS office once the wagons are detached.

The wagon is loaded, released and ready for despatch

Once it is known how much timber is to travel by rail, it can be loaded onto the OBA. The chargeman at the yard is now aware that the timber has been loaded: he also knows the quantity and its destination. He informs the TOPS office at Middlesbrough, who, in turn, release this information to TOPS. This also triggers off the 'consign through TOPS' accounting procedures and the customer's details are married up to the wagon.

The chargeman now places a label on the wagon's solebar. This shows the date, the type of load, its point of origin, the destination and the name of the consignee. It may be argued that a true, dedicated system for wagon movements, which TOPS is, should have no place for pieces of paper stuck on the sides of wagons since all this information is held on computer. A moot point, perhaps!

The date is 21st January 1988, Thornaby Class 08, number 08774 is working the 9P75 trip and is despatched to Middlesbrough Goods to collect traffic for Tees Yard. The 9P75 trip serves the public delivery sidings at Middlesbrough Goods, the private sidings of Cobra Railfreight Ltd, the Blue Circle Cement terminal and A.V. Dawson's private sidings. Wagon number 110798 is laden with timber and ready for collection, as is 110716. Both are bound for the same location. In liaison with the yard planner, the

chargeman informs the TOPS office in which order the wagons will leave the terminal. No. 110716 is behind the locomotive with 110798 bringing up the rear.

The wagon departs for the yard

The trip departs for the yard and again TOPS is informed in order to update the computer of its departure time and the departure time of each wagon in the consist. TOPS also knows how long the trip to Tees Yard should take.

The trip arrives at the yard and the wagons are shunted for train formation

The chargeman at Tees Yard notifies the TOPS office when the wagons arrive. The yard planner is responsible for arranging the formation of the twelve Speedlink departures from Tees. The 'up' sidings, Nos 9-21, are normally used for the Speedlink departures. The yard planner informs the chargeman which siding each wagon will stand in and in what order the wagons will be placed. In this case the two OBAs are in siding 14 of the 'up' yard. (See accompanying figure.) At this early stage they are the only wagons occupying the siding.

The TOPS information now shows the letter L signifying that the wagon is loaded, and LH is the wagon length in feet. The weight WGT is included as is the brake force BF of

```
USER SET U09        -  000000

   SQ WGN NUMBER CL L TFB LH WGT BF DESTN SPL HD COMDTY TAG C
    1 7058990954    L PIA 48 080 43 78512       ISHRCL 77L   NHL*
    2 7058990967    L PIA 48 080 43 78512       ISHRCL 77L   NHL*

USER SET U10        -  000000

   SQ WGN NUMBER CL L TFB LH WGT BF DESTN SPL HD COMDTY TAG C
    1  210448       L VGA 47 047 29 09174       MMWDPL 092   DNL*
    2  210567       L VGA 47 047 29 09174       MMWDPL 092   DNL*
    3  210616       L VGA 47 047 29 09174       MMWDPL 092   DNL*
    4  210493       L VGA 47 047 29 09174       MMWDPL 092   DNL*

USER SET U14        -  000060

   SQ WGN NUMBER CL L TFB LH WGT BF DESTN SPL HD COMDTY TAG C
    1  110716       L OBA 53 029 16 76368       MMTRND 76C
    2  110798       L OBA 53 029 16 76368       MMTRND 76C

USER SET U15        -  000000

   SQ WGN NUMBER CL L TFB LH WGT BF DESTN SPL HD COMDTY TAG C
    1  951133       L BDA 55 055 29 35511 DNL   ISSBRD 355   DNL*
    2 B 923350      L BCW 48 040 09 35511       ISSBRD 355
    3  950987       L BDA 55 048 25 35511       ISSBRD 355
    4  951023       L BDA 55 049 25 35511       ISSBRD 355   DNL*
    5  950629       L BDA 55 046 40 35511       ISSBRD 355   DNL*
    6 B 787539      R RRB 39 012 10 35511 RUB   BARUWS 355
    7  950274       L BDA 55 053 40 35511       ISSBRD 355   DNL*
    8  950403       L BDA 55 051 40 35511       ISSBRD 355   DNL*
    9  950622       L BDA 55 050 40 35511       ISSBRD 355   DNL*
   10  950889       L BDA 55 051 26 35511       ISSBRD 355   DNL*

USER SET U16        -  000000

   SQ WGN NUMBER CL L TFB LH WGT BF DESTN SPL HD COMDTY TAG C
    1  350429       E VEA 22 009 04 74554              74V
    2  350451       E VEA 22 009 04 74554              74V
SHUNTING COMPLETED             TIME

END
```

The TOPS print-out shows that Nos 110716 and 110798 are the only two wagons in user set U14. As the day progresses more wagons will be added to make up the train.

16 tonnes for the loaded OBA. The destination 76368 is the TOPS code referring to Hereford Barrscourt — Western Softwoods. The commodity MMTRND refers to "timber — round" and the TAG is a number allocated to the traffic which informs where that portion of the train will be detached. In this case 76C is the tag number for East Usk near Newport in Gwent.

The yard planner has decided that the two OBAs will go forward on the 17.40 departure. 6O49 Tees to Eastleigh service. The Speedlink office at York reserves space on the 6O49 for the OBAs and is then in a position to inform Western Softwoods that their wagons are booked on the service and will be at their destination next morning.

The Speedlink trains are marshalled according to their tag numbers. This is where TOPS comes into its own. Pre-fed information held permanently on the computer sounds alarm bells if two incompatible loads are marshalled next to each other. If this happens, the yard planner can remarshal the train within the tag numbers or put one of the wagons on another train bound for the same location.

Total weights have already been established by Railfreight and have been fed into the computer. If more wagons are added, warning bells will again sound.

Just before departure a train list is issued. (See accompanying figure.) This gives the full details of the train, including the type of locomotive to be used. In this case it is a Class 47, No. 47309. The hazard column refers to dangerous goods being transported. The code would be passed to control if anything untoward should happen to these wagons. The actual weight of the train is shown, as is the authorised weight of 1,280 tonnes. The reason that this train is running light is that there is more traffic to be picked up and none to set down. The authorised speed limit of the train is 60mph. The tag column shows that the first 16 wagons will be detached at Bescot (652), the next five, including Nos 110798 and 110716 will be detached at Bescot for East Usk (76C), the next three at Oxford (74V) and the last two will travel all the way to Eastleigh (682). In addition, the first tag should be Tinsley but there is no traffic to detach. There will, however, be traffic to add.

```
SPEEDLINK

WTT NO        6049C              TIME  ' 1740    DATE ------

FROM    TEES YARD               TO      EASTLGHYD

     SQ WGN NUMBER CL TPB   LH   WEIGHT   BF SPL HD DESTN R C HAZARD TAG

                   09 SETOUT 86090
                   47309   X         117.000  60
                   18.NO.21.UP.YD.
Z  01 PR    55206   TTA  30  159.910   83  DAN M 65905      1230IA 652
Z  02 ICIA 54354    TTA  60  205.210  112  DAN M 65905      1230IA 652
Z  03 PR    55237   TTA  90  248.140  135  DAN M 65905      1230IA 652
Z  04 ICIA 54374    TTA 120  293.400  164  DAN M 65905      1230IA 652
   05      200745    VDA 157  309.650  171        69411            652
   06      201012    VDA 194  325.800  179        69411            652
   07      210265    VDA 231  342.050  187        69411            652
   08      210292    VDA 268  358.300  195        69411            652
   09      460118    SPA 306  401.850  220      S 65736            652
   10      460505    SPA 344  444.650  245      S 65736            652
   11      460473    SPA 382  487.400  270      S 65736            652
   12      460536    SPA 420  531.300  296      S 65736            652
   13      460578    SPA 458  575.200  321      S 65736            652
   14      460344    SPA 496  619.800  347      S 65736            652
   15      460047    SPA 534  664.350  373      S 65736            652
   16      460132    SPA 572  708.150  399      S 65736            652
   17      950742    BDA 628  770.436  439      M 76361            76C
   18      110716    OBA 666  799.286  455        76368            76C
   19      110798    OBA 704  828.136  471        76368            76C
   20      210585    VGA 751  853.686  489      M 76364            76C
   21      201096    VDA 788  875.656  501        76364            76C
   22      201094    VDA 825  897.814  512        74554            74V
   23      230429    VEA 847  906.414  517        74554            74V
   24      230451    VEA 869  915.014  521        74554            74V
Z  25 ICIA 54373    TTA 899  959.354  550  DAN M 86088      1230IA 862
Z  26 PR    58153   TTA 929 1003.294  579  DAN M 86088      1230IA 862
                        1003.294 TONNES  929 FT       579 POT AIR B/F
   WARNING-Z-DANGEROUS GOODS ON TRAIN - SEE WM P3 AND NOTE COMMENTS BELOW.
           'IN THE EVENT OF ANY OF THE WAGONS CONVEYING DANGEROUS GOODS ON
           THIS TRAIN BEING INVOLVED IN AN ACCIDENT OR AFFECTED BY ANY DEFECT
              BRAKES BINDING, LEAKING VALVES ETC.) ENSURE THAT INFORMATION IS
              PASSED TO THE CONTROL IN RESPECT OF THE SIX CHARACTER EMERGENCY
              CODE.'
       WARNING 30 FT BARR REQ BETWEEN WAGON 26 (DG REF 3.A   ) & REAR OF TRN
              UNLESS ELECTRIC TAIL LAMP PROVIDED

           TRAIN LIST ACCEPTED SEE WM P6 C2/3,C3/7.

THE RULE BOOK SECTION H CLAUSES 4.3.1 & 6.3
CARRIED OUT AND TRAIN IN GOOD ORDER TO PROCEED


PREPARED BY                       SIGNED DEPOT              GRADE
ISSUED AT TEES YARD               SUPVR VALIDATION


----------------------------------------------------------------------
AUTHORISED                          ACTUAL
MAX LOAD        1280 TNNS         1004 TNNS ACTUAL LOAD
OR : -
NUMBER OF WAGONS 0                  26 NUMBER OF WAGONS
BRAKE FORCE TYPE  E1              .... TNNS BRAKE FORCE AVAILABLE(AIR)
FOR ACTUAL LOAD- 296 TNNS           8 HIGHEST R/A IN TRAIN
R/A             8                  929 £ FEET ACT LENGTH    45 SLU
LENGTH LIMIT   0060 SLU
LOCO CLASS      47                  60 MPH MAX TRAIN SPEED
                                    0 PIPED VEHS IN POTENTIAL
                                      BRAKED PORTION OF TRAIN
          TRAIN SINGLE PIPED FROM -----
                                    £ = EXCL. POWER LOCO(S)
======================================================================
```

Just prior to the Speedlink train (6O49) departing, a 'train list' is issued that shows the complete make up of the train, and a copy is handed to the driver.

British Steel operate these Standard Wagon built PGA hoppers on the limestone trains from Redmire to Redcar. Note the apparatus to automatically open and close the bottom doors for the mgr type discharge.

The wagon leaves the yard on the Speedlink train

The driver first checks the train list, then his train, since it is one-man operated. It is then ready for the off. As soon as the train departs, TOPS is informed and the consist is automatically generated for the next yard. This process is repeated until the final destination is reached. The customer's invoice is generated at the same time and the charging process starts automatically.

A customer may wish to know where his wagon is at any given time. TOPS is updated as the train passes various locations and its arrival and departure times at every yard are also fed into TOPS. The customer can then be informed where his wagon is, if it is on time, and when he can expect it. It is interesting to note that on the West Coast Main Line TOPS is updated automatically when a train passes a signal. This system of Automatic Train Reporting (ATR) will be adopted on the East Coast Main Line when electrification is complete.

The wagon arrives at the yard

As soon as our OBA wagons arrive at Bescot, TOPS is updated. The wagons are detached from the train and go forward on the 6V14 Whitemoor to East Usk Speedlink service. This train is due to arrive at East Usk at 07.30 hours. On arrival the two OBAs will go forward on the 6B51 trip from East Usk to Moreton-on-Lugg, arriving at Hereford at 10.20 hours. The wagons can then be emptied and the timber delivered by road on its last leg to Western Softwoods. When the OBAs have been unloaded, TOPS is again updated and the computer automatically prints a final invoice for the company. TOPS then generates disposal instructions and informs control at Bristol exactly where the wagons are needed next. The whole process begins again. Every wagon on the network is monitored in this way and Speedlink services, with only one or two geographical exceptions, arrive within 24 hours of the journey commencing.

Forty six tonne gross OTA wagons with side stanchions, are also used for carrying timber from Middlesbrough and Hexham.

This TTB 46 tonne tank wagon, painted light blue with the operator's name on the side, is used to convey resin from Duxford to Egger UK at Hexham.

Forty three of these 45 tonne gross PCA wagons were acquired by British Alcan under a Section 8 grant. They convey alumina from Blyth to Lochaber (Fort William). Eventually they will replace the old grain wagons currently being used.

Vacuum-braked freights are now diminishing. These vacuum-braked MSV wagons are still used on the Peak Forest – Leeds Peakstone trains.

British Steel owned iron ore tippler wagon No. 26000 built by BR at Shildon in 1971, is fitted with rotary buckeye couplings. Wagons like this are not only used between Immingham and Scunthorpe, but also carry the dolofines from Thrislington to Ravenscraig.

This TTA tank wagon conveys bitumen and is owned by Shell U.K. The wagons are fitted with chimneys for when the flame tubes are lit to heat the oil.

Wagon Type Codes

Wagon type codes consist of three characters the first two of which identify the general vehicle type, the third character denoting the brake type.

eg   MDO = Mineral, side doors 21.5t unfitted.
     MDV = Mineral, side doors 21.5t vac. brake.

Vehicle Brake Type Codes

A   Air brake
B   Air brake & vacuum pipe
F   A.F.I. brake
G   A.F.I. brake and air pipe
H   Dual brake (A.F.I. & air)
O   Unfitted
P   Piped (vacuum)
Q   Piped (air)
R   Piped (dual)
V   Vacuum brake
W   Vacuum brake and air pipe
X   Dual brake (vacuum & air)

TOPS Code	Vehicle Description

Steel Carrying – Bogie

BA   Bogie Steel AB 40ft 77.5 – 78.5t
BB   Bogie Steel AB 50ft 73.5 – 75.5t
BC   Bogie Bolster C 30.5t
BD   Bogie Bolster D 42.5 – 58t
BE   Bogie Bolster E 32.5t
BF   Bogie Steel Carrier 54t
BG   Bogie Strip Coil G Nylon Hood 44.5t
BJ   Bogie Strip Coil E Nylon Hood 44.5t
BL   Bogie Bolster – Disc Brakes 57t
BM   Bogie Plate E. Wide Body 58.5t
BN   Bogie Strip Coil K Nylon Hood 61t
BP   Bogie Plate E 42.5 – 58.5t
BQ   Bogie Bolster Q 30.5 – 31.5t
BS   Bogie Timber 42.5t
BT   Bogie Bolster T 31t
BV   Bogie Strip Coil V, Nylon Hood 61t
BX   Trestle Plate AB, ED 42.5t
BY   Bogie Strip Coil T. Nylon Hood 61t

Covered Bulk Carriers

CB   Covhop AB 31 – 31.5t
CH   Covhop 24.5t
CP   Presflo 20.5 – 22.5t
CB   Fly Ash 21.5t

Flats

FB   Conflat AB 25.5t
FE   Conflat E 42.5 – 46t
FF   Freightliner Inner 52 – 62t
FG   Freightliner Outer 52 – 62t
FH   Lowliner 49 – 63t
FJ   Freightliner 60' with buffers & drawgear
FM   Freight Flat 42 – 60.3t
FN   Flatrol Atomic Flask 56t
FO   Conflat P (ex SAA), coal 31.2t
FQ   Cartic
FR   Transformer MC 135t
FU   Bogie container wagon
FV   Carflat 10t
FW   Bogie flat 17 – 42.5t
FY   Bogie Container Wagon

Hoppers

HA   Coal hopper (MGR) 32.5t
HB   Coal hopper, gravity discharge, 45mph ety
HD   Coal hopper 32.8t
HE   Coal hopper, gravity discharge, 60mph ety
HJ   Ironstone hopper 24.5t
HK   Ironstone hopper 33.5t
HT   Coal hopper 21.5 – 25t
HU   Coal hopper 24.5 – 25t

International Ferry Wagons

IC   Tanks, all types, 23 – 80t
IF   Flats, incl. bogie flats 15 – 45.5t
II   Interfrigo 17 – 25.6t
IL   Vans, large, incl. bogie, 21.5 – 54t
IM   Vans, medium, incl. sliding roof and insulated 20 – 27.5t
IO   Open high 27.5 – 29.5t
IP   Privately owned vehicles (all types except tanks) 20 – 105t
IT   Transfesa 25 – 27t
IX   Bogie well 39 – 59t

Mineral (incl. hoppered)

MC   Min. 16.5t
MD   Min. 21.5t
MS   Tippler, ironstone 26.5t
MT   Tippler, ironstone 24t
MX   Min. 16.5t (push type brakes)

Open

OA   Open AB 31.5t
OB   Open AB (turnover bolster) 30.5 – 31.5t
OC   Open AB wth bolster 31.5t
OD   Open AB (MOD) 12t
OE   Open AB (hooded)
OJ   High (ex ferry) 21.5t
OO   China clay 13t
OT   Timber 31t
OU   Shockhood B 22.5t

Privately Owned Wagons (excl. Tanks)

PA   Covered bulk (Covhop, Grain, Lime) 23 – 36t
PB   Covered bulk (bogie) 63 – 71t
PC   Cement, 2 axle 22 – 36.5t
PD   Presflo bogie 63 – 79.6t
PE   Bulk powder, tip air, two axle
PF   Bogie flats (Weltrol, Carflat) 10 – 50t
PG   Hopper, two axle (Aggregate, Ironstone, Salt, Gypsum) 32.8 – 38.8t
PH   Hopper, bogie (Aggregate, Ballast, Limestone) 28 – 81.9t
PI   Privately owned RIV (Covhop, Well wagon, Coil) 28 – 116t
PJ   Cartic 8t
PK   Artic, 3 axle 14t
PL   2 tier car carrier 12t
PM   Mineral, no doors 23 – 25.7t
PN   Open, bogie, pallet 40t
PO   Open, scrap, 2 axle 35.1 – 37.3t
PP   Weedkilling/Escort coach 2.5 – 15t
PQ   Autic 3 axle 8 – 10t
PR   China clay, curtain roof 22.3 – 25.3t
PS   Ironstone tippler, 2 axle 21.2 – 39.5t
PT   Ironstone tippler, bogie 60 – 77.5t
PV   Van (incl. Palvan) 2 axle 22.5 – 31.8t
PW   Palvan, bogie 43.5 – 48t
PX   Misc. vehicles incl. Match, Flask, Ramp, Flatrol, Coil, Tube, Bogie bolster

Railway Operating Vehicles
CA Traffic brake van (all types)
RB Barrier
RF F/Liner, Tippler, LTE adaptors
RG Freightliner adaptor
RH Tippler adaptor
RR Runner

Steel Carrying – 2 Axle
SC Strip coil C 24.5t
SD Bolster (Ex plate) 31t
SE Rod coil (Ex plate) 22.5t
SF Strip coil A, nylon hood 21.5t
SG Strip coil B, nylon hood. 24.5t
SH Strip coil (Ex plate) 31.5t
SJ Strip coil J (Ex tippler) 24.5t
SK Rod coil (Ex plate) 29.5t
SO Pipe 12.2t
SP Plate, pig iron 22.5 – 29t
SR Rod coil R (Ex plate) 24.5t
ST Tube 22.5t
SU Coil U, Ex Shockhood 20.5t

Tank, Privately Owned
TC Tank bogie 80 – 89t
TD Tank bogie 90 – 99t
TE Tank bogie 100t
TI Tank 2 axle/bogie RIV
TM Tank 3 axle 25t
TR Tank 2 axle 20 – 29t
TS Tank 2 axle 30 – 39t
TT Tank 2 axle 40 – 49t
TU Tank 2 axle 50 – 59t

Vans (Covered – General Merchandise)
VA Van, full length doors, ventilated, 60 mph, 20.5 – 30t
VB Van, full length doors, non ventilated, 60 mph, 28.5 – 29.5t
VC Van, centre door, non ventilated. 60 mph, 29 – 30.5t
VD Van, centre/end cupboard doors, non ventilated 25t
VE Van, vanwide, MOD (roller bearings) 12t
VF Van, MOD (Ex vanwide, roller bearings) fitted with alarm. 11.5t
VG Van, full length doors, non ventilated 28 – 29t
VH Van, curtain sides 25t
VJ Van AB (Ex RIV) 25t

Continental Ferry Wagon Administration Registration Numbers
These are the 3rd and 4th digits of the painted wagon number (1st and 2nd digits on the wagon file)

No.	Owning Administration	Initials
44	Budapest Local Railway	BHEV
54	Czechoslovakian State Railways	CSD
55	Hungarian State Railways*	MAV
70	British Rail	BR
71	Spanish National Railway Co. (includes Transfesa wagons)	RENFE
72	Jugoslavian Railways	JZ
74	Swedish State Railways	SJ
80	German Federal Railways*	DB
81	Austrian Federal Railways*	OBB
83	Italian State Railways*	FS
85	Swiss Federal Railways*	CFF
87	French State Railways*	SNCF
88	Belgian National Railway Co.	SNCB

*Also operate Interfrigo wagons

Some of these wooden bodied Transfesa wagons are used for carrying pure terephthalic acid (PTA) from ICI Wilton via the train ferries to Spain and Portugal.

Chapter 10

Speedlink

The problems of the wagonload system were well known by the 1960s. However, since there was quite a lot of revenue being earned by the network, no decision was taken at that time to dispense with it. When in the 1970s the question came to be asked again, it was decided that there must be a wagonload system to support the trainload system. It would not be in British Rail's interest to have a trainload-only railway. That wagonload system had to be modern, air-braked, 60mph, in new wagons and increasingly they would be private-owner wagons. The service would not be 'anywhere to anywhere' as before, but tailor-made for particular transits grouped together into trains where they could follow a common route. Coming into being in 1974 it was to be a disciplined and cost-effective organisation.

As there was still a lot of the traditional wagonload system about in vacuum-braked or unbraked wagons, passing through hump yards which were built in the 1950s and 1960s it started off slowly. In fact, it took ten years, from 1974 to 1984, when the traditional wagonload service was finally abandoned, to cut over to the Speedlink that we know today. Even then there were two traffics which had not managed to convert themselves to Speedlink because there were no suitable air-braked wagons available. One was distributive coal, the other scrap. After 1984 they had their own system for moving the traffic, independent of Speedlink until the 60mph air-braked wagons were ready and they could be superimposed upon the Speedlink system. This took a further twelve months and even today some movements on Tyneside involving scrap still have an element of mixed working.

The idea was to run wagons the maximum distance without marshalling. Marshalling yards were no longer to be for assembling wagons into trainloads and dispersing them from trainloads to a variety of destinations. They were to be for portion-exchanging. The trains today are sectionised, that is, they arrive in a yard with up to seven or eight

On 9th October 1987 No. 31442 heads the trip to Hexham out of Tyne Yard. It conveys a resin wagon, bogie oil wagon and scrap metal MDW wagons.

No. 08441 shunts VGA wagons loaded with Guinness from Park Royal into the Tyneside Central Freight Depot.

On 18th June 1987, No. 31289 enters Tyne Yard with the 6P02 trip from Elswick and TCFD. As well as empty Guinness kegs in the VGAs it conveys bitumen tank wagons from Colas Roads returning to Shell at Stanlow.

No. 47310 approaches Eaglescliffe on 15th August 1988 with the 7M85 Tees – Bescot Speedlink service.

On the evening of 10th February 1987, No. 37158 departs from Tees Yard with the 6V66 Speedlink train conveying containerised potash for ICI at Severnside.

sections. It is now a question of cutting into these sections and allocating them to other trains or of putting them aside for local distribution. The effects of this method of working can be seen at yards all over the country. Staffing levels have dropped and the hump has gone since there is no relevance for hump-shunting in the sectionising described. At Tees this has taken some time and only now are the operations beginning to contract down into a small part of the premises. Certainly if British Rail were starting to build yards again, a space no larger than 20-30% of the original surface area would be required.

Tyne Yard has taken rather longer and reorganisation is being done on the back of electrification and resignalling. When completed it will have contracted down into 30% of the original area. Although Speedlink will use electric traction on the ECML, the final pattern of electric haulage has still to be determined. It will, however, be possible to haul the trains all the way from Willesden via Doncaster and Tyne yards to Millerhill. Tinsley is a supporting yard to Doncaster and is for trains that do not need to go into Doncaster, and fulfils two roles. It deals with traffic from the Sheffield area, which is primarily scrap, and there is a degree of portion-exchanging on the NE — SW axis.

The Doncaster Belmont Speedlink yard is unfortunately very limited in space. Situated south of the station, a train arriving on the SW — NE axis has to turn south having come from the Sheffield direction. If it is going north on the ECML, it has to reverse before doing so. The size of the yard is such that British Rail cannot cope with too much of that! Tees Yard, though not on the main line, is vitally important in the servicing of a large catchment of terminals in the Teesside area. It is accessed from both north and south.

At first it was thought that locomotive dedication was only suited to the trainload business but later thinking brought Speedlink into line with the rest of Railfreight. This was needed in order that Speedlink should have its own locomotives which were not to be competed for by other parts of Railfreight. It was also an advantage to have

No. 37510 collects the afternoon traffic from Stockton Haulage at Middlesbrough to be tripped back to Tees Yard.

No. 08504 shunts BDA wagons with steel sections from Lackenby into a train at Tees Yard.

locomotives engineered for the particular characteristics of the trains they were running. Speedlink trunk trains can have trailing loads of between 1,200 and 1,400 tonnes. Although not the heaviest on the system, they do travel at up to 60mph over quite long distances all over the country. It was also recognised that if locomotives which are doing a similar sort of work receive maintenance at the same place by the same technical staff, this was superior to the common-user arrangement. Speedlink therefore has a closer control over the cost of the operation and it could also be cheaper. Even if it is not, it will avoid more costs being placed upon the Speedlink network than it deserves to pick up! The outcome is that British Rail has put most of its main line locomotives into Tinsley, a depot at a strategic point in the network since a lot of Speedlink trains pass through or near to the area. Apart from its excellent geographic location — no other major traction depot is so well situated — Tinsley has a very high engineering reputation. From May 1988 the allocation was 25 Class 31s, 34 x 37s and 110 x 47s. There are also odd pockets of locomotives, some of which are not of Speedlink's above-mentioned standard classes: for example, marginal use of Class 33s on the Southern Region and eight Class

26s in Scotland. Obviously it would be wrong to move these locomotives away from the regions where they are maintained. There are also one or two extreme locations of the standard classes — 37s in Cornwall and RETB-fitted 37s in Scotland. Dedication of the fleet means that Speedlink has taken on a lot of responsibility. If there is a shortage of locomotives, Speedlink cannot always count on other sectors to help out. In addition, the locomotives have to be rotated to the Tinsley depot for all their heavy maintenance schedules. Although light inspections and refuelling can be had anywhere on the system, significant engineering attention must be done at base to obtain the continuity and the subsequent quality. The 110 Class 47s will cover 85 diagrams. To protect the diagrams, at least 88 locomotives in good order will be required every day, leaving 22 under maintenance. What is looked for here is the number of locomotives to meet diagram commitments and improved standards of reliability.

Let us now consider the various areas of the North East region and the traffics involved. Although Tyneside is not a particularly heavy originating and receiving area for domestic traffic, Tyne Yard still has a significant role in dealing

No. 37507 Hartlepool Pipe Mill passes Cowpen Bewley on 28th June 1988 with the morning trip working, conveying Reed paper from Linkflow at Hartlepool.

One of British Sugar's two Ruston & Hornsby 0-4-0 diesel-mechanical shunters stands on the end of molasses wagons whilst they are loaded at York. The wagons will go forward on Speedlink for Distillers at Menstrie.

No. 47286 heads the afternoon feeder service from Scunthorpe to Doncaster past Medge Hall on 23rd April 1987.

On a misty 7th April 1987, No. 08516 reverses the soda ash wagons into the Rockware Glass sidings at Knottingley.

On 4th August 1988, No. 47311 *Warrington Yard heads north past Ryther with the Doncaster – Aberdeen Speedlink train.*

No. 31248 *arrives at Belmont Yard with the trip from Plasmor's sidings at Heck on 22nd June 1987.*

On Thursday 11th August 1988 *the Hunslet (Leeds) – Tinsley Speedlink service consisted of an empty BDA wagon and a POA scrap wagon from Crossley Evans at Shipley. Hauling the train is No. 31145.*

with interchange as it is at the crossroads of the Teesside traffic to the West Coast and the East Coast Main Line. At present there does not seem to be much growth potential for Speedlink in the area, although what business there is makes it attractive enough for Speedlink to want to keep it. The main centres of activity are Tyne Central Freight Depot which handles a wide range of goods, and Colas Roads (Jobling Purser). Timber traffic also passes through from Hexham on its way down to Wales and to Norfolk. Timber is one of the traffics which British Rail and Speedlink have won a way back into, after several years without any handling.

Occasional loads of steel plate are received from Scunthorpe for shipbuilding. Once a steady flow, this has now been hit by the decline of the industry on Tyneside. Egger UK Ltd receives chemicals traffic from Ciba-Geigy at Duxford and chipboard from Austria. There is also a variable volume of grain from Tweedmouth. Scrap traffic passes from Southwick, Dunstan and Bladon to Lackenby. An important flow from Steetley's quarries around Ferryhill is

agricultural lime, mostly to the east of Scotland. Redland Rooftiles also receive products at their siding at Gateshead.

Moving down to Teesside, there is a significant flow of steel to the West Midlands, and Linkflow of Hartlepool has in the past received imported steel at their siding from the docks and forwarded it as required. A fair amount of scrap also moves on Teesside from Thompson's of Stockton to Sheffield, and Herring's of Hartlepool also forward to the Sheffield area as part of the Standard Railfreight Scrap Scheme. Some bagged fertiliser is forwarded by ICI to Middlesbrough Goods for a wide range of destinations. There is a constant flow of potash and salt from Boulby Mine, and ICI at Billingham and Wilton provide a variety of chemicals traffic. Linkflow also handles Reed paper, much of which goes to Carlisle.

The volume of traffic at York dropped when Rowntrees decided no longer to use rail, but there is a seasonal flow of molasses from the British Sugar Corporation to Distillers at Menstrie. Sugar beet nuts are sent from York to Carnforth and local departmental traffic is also carried by Speedlink.

On 2nd September 1987, No. 47219 on the 6O49 Tees to Eastleigh (with tanks) and No 47142 with the 7H80 Doncaster to Bescot, pause at Tinsley whilst portions of the train are taken off and others added.

In the North Humberside area there is an interesting movement from BP at Saltend, which is actually trainload but goes via the Speedlink network. From Hull the train goes to Tinsley. One part travels on to Baglan Bay in West Wales and the balance is Speedlink-forwarded to Spondon. The Purfleet-Haverton Hill sections come out of Hull on a separate trip and are dispersed at Doncaster. Goole also sees some steel and fertiliser traffic but automotives, which were formerly the backbone here, now only pass on an irregular basis to Stranraer and Leith because of a change in Renault's distribution arrangements.

Rockware at Wheatley, Doncaster takes in soda ash from Northwich and there is also a movement of limestone from Hindlow to Wheatley. Plasmor of Heck send their building materials to Biggleswade and Bow and are certainly one of Speedlink's success stories. On occasions extra trains have to be put on to accommodate the volume of traffic. The other major revenue-earning traffic in the area stems from BREL in Doncaster. In recent times Doncaster has become increasingly important both as a trunk interchange location and as a focal point from trip services that run in the area to Hunslet, Goole and Scunthorpe.

In Leeds there is steel traffic to D & F Steels and Dunlop & Ranken, as well as scrap from Crossley's at Shipley. Whitehall Road handles soft drinks, steel to a limited degree and some international business. Hunslet, the Leeds local area yard, is operated on a single shift, requiring all business to be done between 06.30 and 14.30. A direct service operates from Willesden to Hunslet, conveying cars for the Wrenthorpe Terminal and also scrap empties from Tinsley. A Doncaster service in the morning takes the traffic not routed via Tinsley. At Wakefield, Cobra Railfreight deal with traffic from Allied Steel & Wire in Cardiff, timber, shoddy in Transfesa wagons for Portugal, wine and blast grit. Procor at Horbury Junction have an extensive wagon repair undertaking which uses Speedlink services and Redland Rooftiles have an activity at Dewsbury Railway Street. Speedlink also carries departmental traffic such as spares and fuel oil.

In the Sheffield and Rotherham area, steel is the main commodity in terms of originating and received traffic. There are significant flows on Speedlink to the West Midlands, some to South Wales and general merchandise passes through Sheffield Freight Centre. Tinsley is now important, having assumed Dringhouses' role in the interchange of train sections. This is in addition to its own locally generated traffic, most of which is steel.

In the Scunthorpe area there is the inevitable steel traffic to a wide variety of destinations. The principal flows are to Mossend, Stranraer, West Midlands, South Wales, Hereford and the West Country. There is also a flow of Rugby Portland cement out of Scunthorpe Goods Yard to Halling in Kent and the company has in the past forwarded to Rugby, Bow, Beeston and Ardwick. As the result of very significant changes in the cement market, it is unlikely that the latter four traffics will resume in the near future.

Immingham is a very productive Speedlink area. The marshalling yard is owned by the Docks Board but with British Rail pilots and drivers. There are major flows of fertiliser from Norsk Hydro to an assortment of destinations — Fishguard, Shrewsbury, Carlisle, Aberdeen and possibly to Holton Heath in Dorset when it opens. Chemicals traffic out of Immingham Storage goes to Scotland, and Immingham Railfreight Terminal, at the east gate of Immingham Dock, has extensive storage facilities.

They handle large quantities of steel and store steel traffic out of Scunthorpe. Saab cars have also been handled. The local firm of SCM brings in goods by road and these are transferred to rail for forwarding on Speedlink. The large oil refineries of Total & Petrofina and Humber Oil also send product out for Speedlink distribution.

Grimsby does not generate much Speedlink traffic. It was hoped to win the Mallaig fish traffic and a well-publicised trial operation was mounted. Routed via Mossend, Carlisle and Tyne, the movement was both trainload and Speedlink. The fish came down trainload and the empties went back Speedlink. Although pronounced a success at the time, nothing has yet developed from it.

Paul's Grain of Gainsborough send grain via Speedlink through the area but it is, by its very nature, seasonal. A fairly widespread activity on Speedlink is the movement of MOD traffic. The vans used are mainly VEAs with some VDAs, and the Warwells and Warflats are for vehicular traffic.

Speedlink's main problem has been one of profitability. Whilst it is subsidised by the more profitable parts of Railfreight, the situation is delicate. If, however, it is viewed that there should not be any part of Railfreight which is not profitable, that is, that there should be no internal cross-subsidy, Speedlink would find it very demanding. A slimming of services has already taken place, the number of trunk trains being somewhat lower than the 150 which once ran. Certainly since 1986 Speedlink has become more specialised and has ceased to go to some of the more remote places unless there is a real strength of flow. Fortunately Speedlink has been able to achieve almost all of its cost reductions without overboarding any business. In the cases where it has been necessary to cease serving a particular location, that business has mainly transferred to other places, so that in net terms there has been little reduction. A further problem has been Speedlink's inability to compete on price, this being due in the main to road haulage becoming increasingly more productive with its larger vehicles.

A problem always likely to crop up is the quality of the service. Speedlink traffic is time-sensitive traffic, and therefore has to run to tight schedules. In some trainload movements, for example, coal and aggregates, there is some stockpile in the operation, and if the train does not arrive on time, the customer can still carry on business. He is unlikely to lose money and can make up the loss of tonnage later. In many instances the Speedlink product is perishable in that it is purpose-made of individual transits. There is a precise start time and placement time for every traffic and the tolerance can be quite small in some cases, as little as half an hour. The common trend is to have to achieve punctual presentation for the customer either because of the contents of the vehicles or the need to turn the wagons round quickly. Therefore, locomotive failure, track circuit problems, wires that come down, broken rails etc, make Speedlink very vulnerable. If customers would accept a tolerance of one hour, better still two hours, the net result would obviously be better and Speedlink would not be so exposed to the quite minor disruptions that can occur.

Speedlink's aim is to achieve 19 out of 20 transits — that is all but one day every four weeks — within customer tolerance. This tolerance figure could be half an hour, one or two hours. The figure is immaterial. What matters is the placement of the traffic before or on time, so that the customer is not inconvenienced in any way. A disruption to his business one day in twenty is as good as, if not better than, any other form of transport, and he is likely to accept that.

New traction will certainly help Speedlink achieve its aims, and if there was any doubt about the future of the service, it has been dispelled by the building of the Channel Tunnel. It is now essential that no action be taken which will worsen rail's position when the Tunnel opens. Although most of the freight traffic through the Tunnel will be trainload, the wagonload, or perhaps more accurately, the less-than-trainload operation, is reckoned to amount to approximately a quarter to a third of the freight activity. This figure is constantly being re-thought and it may be that these early forecasts of the proportion of wagonload to trainload are underestimating the strength of wagonload flows. After all, many producers will not be able to despatch goods in trainload quantities, 100-300 tonnes being far more within their capability. Certainly the distances from the North of England to the Continent should make Speedlink very competitive as they will be much in excess of the 250 miles* where it is generally reckoned that rail becomes cheaper than road. The Tunnel could well be the spur to improving Speedlink's fortunes.

*With heavier specialised traffics the figure can be as low as 200 miles, but with light and highly time-sensitive traffics, which require a very precise movement, this figure might be 400 miles plus.

Speedlink Network

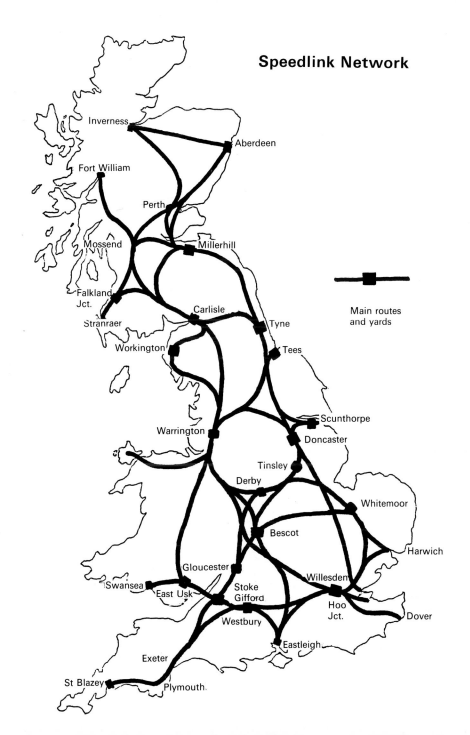

Main routes and yards

Chapter 11

The Road Ahead

It may seem paradoxical that a nation which once had the best railway system in Europe, arguably in the world, and a fine railway tradition reaching well into this century, could have come to a point where in 1985/86 it handled only 9% (1) of the freight moved in the country. Regrettable though this may be, the causes are not difficult to find and have been outlined at various points in the book. But what of the future?

The new liveries, the symbols, are Railfreight's way of saying that the old image has been replaced by a new forward-looking one. Strength, pride, confidence and performance are the keystones. Today Railfreight has no inhibitions about its market place. It stretches from the north of Scotland down. The North East is being considered as critically in Railfreight's thinking as other parts of the country and certainly its position favours the longer haul to markets in the South and for international traffic travelling on the new ferry from Dover. In general terms, traffic which is most suited to rail, is most suited to the long haul (2), this being the more densely-loading traffic such as steel and chemicals. This traffic has two characteristics. First, because it is densely-loading, Railfreight can take advantage of high-capacity wagons which can load two and a half times as much as a road vehicle. Second, these commodities tend to be not so critically time-sensitive. The movements are planned, often they are inter-factory movements of dense semi-finished products which go into stock and are drawn from stock. Railfreight virtually becomes a pipeline, part of the production process. Again, the North East is excellently placed here, since steel and chemicals are major industries in the region. As quite a lot of steel still uses coastal shipping, and as Railfreight's share of the chemicals business is relatively small, these are areas for marketing initiatives, especially so with the building of the Channel Tunnel.

A further development which can benefit the North East lies in the growth of intermodal traffic. Interest has already been shown by potential customers in such innovations as the Procor low-loader, Minilink and Tiger Rail's Trailer-Train. The former could go some way to solving the piggy-backing problem within our limited loading gauge, whilst the advantages of the latter two are that this type of demountable or swap-body needs no expensive terminal handling equipment and can be used from virtually any siding which gives access to road vehicles. Again the trunk haul will be by rail, collection and delivery being by road.

As Railfreight is basically the carrier, it is dependent on the economy and on how well its customers are doing. But if the willingness to invest in rail on the part of private terminal operators such as Viking Shipping at Selby, Selby Storage, Stockton Haulage, Smallers, Immingham Railfreight Terminal, A.V. Dawson and Cobra Railfreight is any indication, then Railfreight's new image is not out of place and its optimism is not unfounded. Also, if multi-nationals like CAIB, and major wagon builders and leasers are similarly looking to invest in rail, it has to be assumed that they have done their sums correctly and that the future is bright. For some years, British Rail has been trying to sort out a strategy for Railfreight, and it may be argued that although Railfreight has remained in the market place, the role has been very much a reactive rather than a productive one. Today, however, there is a confidence that Railfreight has a product which can be developed. What is now needed is aggressive and positive marketing, and above all investment.

(1)   Though this is the generally accepted figure, it should be said that the other 91% includes many traffics which are not of interest to Railfreight.
(2)   Short hauls, when intensive, such as in iron ore and mgr coal operations, are the exception to this rule.

New concepts have to be developed to stave off competition, like this PFA flat wagon with four containers for carrying cold reduced coil which is sensitive to the elements. The containers can be unloaded by fork lift trucks.

Private terminal operators are willing to handle anything by rail. Titanium dioxide is loaded onto a Transfesa wagon for movement to the Continent at Immingham Railfreight Terminals Ltd.